YOU CAN'T TAKE IT WITH YOU

A Comedy in Three Acts

by MOSS HART and
GEORGE S. KAUFMAN

★

★

DRAMATISTS
PLAY SERVICE
INC.

"You Can't Take It With You" was produced at the Booth Theatre, New York City, Monday night, December 14th, 1936, by Sam H. Harris, with the following cast:

PENELOPE SYCAMORE .... Josephine Hull
ESSIE .... Paula Trueman
RHEBA .... Ruth Attaway
PAUL SYCAMORE .... Frank Wilcox
MR. DE PINNA .... Frank Conlan
ED .... George Heller
DONALD .... Oscar Polk
MARTIN VANDERHOF .... Henry Travers
ALICE .... Margot Stevenson
HENDERSON .... Hugh Rennie
TONY KIRBY .... Jess Barker
BORIS KOLENKHOV .... George Tobias
GAY WELLINGTON .... Mitzi Hajos
MR. KIRBY .... William J. Kelly
MRS. KIRBY .... Virginia Hammond
THREE MEN .... } George Leach
                                            Ralph Holmes
                                            Franklin Heller
OLGA .... Anna Lubowe

_____

STAGE MANAGER .... William McFadden

The scene is the home of Martin Vanderhof, New York.

ACT I

A Wednesday evening. (During this act the curtain is lowered to denote the passing of several hours.)

ACT II

A week later.

ACT III

The next day.

YOU CAN'T TAKE IT WITH YOU

~~~~~~

ACT I

SCENE 1: *The home of* MARTIN VANDERHOF—*just around the corner from Columbia University, but don't go looking for it. The room we see is what is customarily described as a living room, but in this house the term is something of an understatement. The every-man-for-himself room would be more like it. For here meals are eaten, plays ar written, snakes collected, ballet steps practiced, xylophones played, printing presses operated—if there were room enough there would probably be ice skating. In short, the brood presided over by* MARTIN VANDERHOF *goes on about the business of living in the fullest sense of the word. From* GRANDPA VANDERHOF *down, they are individualists. This is a house where you do as you like, and no questions asked.*

At the moment, GRANDPA VANDERHOF'S *daughter,* MRS. PENELOPE SYCAMORE, *is doing what she likes more than anything else in the world. She is writing a play—her eleventh. Comfortably ensconced in what is affectionately known as Mother's Corner, she is pounding away on a typewriter perched precariously on a rickety card table. Also on the table is one of those plaster-paris skulls ordinarily used as an ash tray, but which serves* PENELOPE *as a candy jar. And, because* PENNY *likes companionship, there are two kittens on the table, busily lapping at a saucer of milk.*

PENELOPE VANDERHOF SYCAMORE *is a round little woman in her early fifties, comfortable looking, gentle, homey. One would not suspect that under that placid exterior there surges the Divine Urge—but it does, it does.*

After a moment her fingers lag on the keys; a thoughtful ex-

pression comes over her face. Abstractedly she takes a piece of candy out of the skull, pops it into her mouth. As always, it furnishes the needed inspiration—with a furious burst of speed she finishes a page and whips it out of the machine. Quite mechanically, she picks up one of the kittens, adds the sheet of paper to the pile underneath, replaces the kitten.

As she goes back to work, ESSIE CARMICHAEL, MRS. SYCA-MORE'S *eldest daughter, comes in from the kitchen. A girl of about twenty-nine, very slight, a curious air of the pixie about her. She is wearing ballet slippers—in fact, she wears them throughout the play.*

ESSIE. (*Enters* U.R. *as* PENNY *crosses back with skull and fanning herself takes paper out of typewriter.*) My, that kitchen's hot.

PENNY. (*Finishing a bit of typing.*) What, Essie? (*Rises and crosses to* R. *a step.*)

ESSIE. (*Crossing to* R. *of table.*) I say the kitchen's awful hot. That new candy I'm making—it just won't ever get cool.

PENNY. Do you have to make candy today, Essie? It's such a hot day.

ESSIE. Well, I got all those new orders. Ed went out and got a bunch of new orders. (*Leg limbering exercise on chair.*)

PENNY. My, if it keeps on I suppose you'll be opening up a store.

ESSIE. That's what Ed was saying last night (*She leans body forward.*), but I said No, I want to be a dancer. (*Points to* C.)

PENNY. (*Returning to her desk.*) The only trouble with dancing is, it takes so long. You've been studying such a long time.

ESSIE. (*Slowly drawing a leg up behind her as she talks.*) Only—eight—years. After all, Mother, you've been writing plays for eight years. We started about the same time, didn't we?

PENNY. Yes, but you shouldn't count my first two years, because I was learning to type. (*At her desk.*)

(*From the kitchen comes a colored maid named* RHEBA—*a very black girl somewhere in her thirties. She carries eight napkins.*)

RHEBA. (*As she enters.*) I think the candy's *hardening up* now, Miss Essie. (*Puts napkins on* U.S. *chair of table.*)

ESSIE. Oh, thanks, Rheba. I'll bring some in, Mother—I want you to try it. (*She goes into kitchen* U.R.)

(PENNY *returns to her work, sits—puts fresh paper in and types— as* RHEBA *removes table centerpiece and goes to buffet.*)

6

RHEBA. (*Taking a tablecloth from buffet drawer.*) Finish the second act, Mrs. Sycamore?

PENNY. Uh? What?

RHEBA. (*Returning to table, she throws tablecloth over back of a chair and removes table cover.*) I said, did you finish the second act?

PENNY. (*Crosses to* R. *a step with script, papers, and pencil.*) Oh, no, Rheba. I've just got Cynthia entering the monastery.

RHEBA. She was at the Kit Kat, wasn't she?

PENNY. (*Crosses to* L. *of table.*) Well, she gets tired of the Kit Kat Club, and there's this monastery, so she goes there.

RHEBA. Do they let her in?

PENNY. Yes, I made it Visitors' Day, so of course anybody can come.

RHEBA. Oh. (*As she spreads tablecloth.*)

PENNY. So she arrives on Visitors' Day, and—just stays.

RHEBA. You mean she stays all night?

PENNY. Oh, yes. She stays six years. (*Crosses to her desk and sits.*)

RHEBA. Six years? (*Starting for kitchen.*) My, I bet she busts that monastery wide open. (*She is gone.*)

PENNY. (*Half to herself, as she types.*) "Six Years Later." . . .

(PAUL SYCAMORE *comes up from the cellar. Mid-fifties, but with a kind of youthful air. His quiet charm and mild manner are distinctly engaging. He is carrying a frying pan containing several small firecrackers. He is smoking a cigarette.*)

PAUL. (*Turning back as he comes through door* D.R.) Mr. De Pinna! (*A voice from below: "Yah?"*) Mr. De Pinna, will you bring up one of those new skyrockets, please? I want to show them to Mrs. Sycamore. (*An answering "Sure!" from cellar as he crosses toward* PENNY, *who rises.*) Look, Penny—what do you think of these little firecrackers we just made? We can sell them ten strings for a cent. Listen. (*He puts one down in the pan on table and lights it. It goes off with a good bang.*) Nice, huh?

PENNY. Yes. Paul, dear, were you ever in a monastery?

PAUL. (*Puts half of firecrackers in pan, quite calmly as he crosses to her.*) No, I wasn't. . . . Wait till you see the new rockets. Gold stars, then blue stars, and then bombs, and then a balloon. Mr. De Pinna thought of the balloon.

(DE PINNA *enters.*)

7

PENNY. Sounds lovely. Did you do all that today? (*Crosses to desk chair.*)

PAUL. Sure. We made up—Oh, here we are. (DE PINNA *comes up from cellar. A bald-headed little man with a serious manner, carrying 2 good-sized skyrockets. He crosses to* PAUL. PAUL *takes one to show* PENNY.) Look, Penny. Costs us eighteen cents to make and we sell 'em for fifty. How many do you figure we can make before the Fourth of July, Mr. De Pinna?

DE PINNA. Well, we've got two weeks yet—what day you going to take the stuff up to Mount Vernon?

PAUL. (*Picking up his pan and firecrackers.*) About a week. You know, we're going to need a larger booth this year—got a lot of stuff made up. (PAUL *starts* R.) Come on, we're not through yet. (DE PINNA *follows.*)

DE PINNA. Look, Mr. Sycamore, (*Examining rocket in his hand.*) I'm afraid the powder chamber is just a little bit close to the balloon.

PAUL. Well, we got the stars and the bombs in between.

DE PINNA. But that don't give the balloon time enough. A balloon needs plenty of time.

PAUL. Come on—come on. Let's go down in the cellar and try it. (*He exits* D.R.)

DE PINNA. (*Starting off.*) All right.

PENNY. (*Rising and crossing two steps* R.) Mr. De Pinna, if a girl you loved entered a monastery, what would you do?

DE PINNA. Oh I don't know, Mrs. Sycamore . . . it's been so long.

(PENNY *sits at her desk, as* DE PINNA *exits* D.R. *She starts to type again as* RHEBA *enters from kitchen bringing a pile of plates and salt and pepper shakers.*)

RHEBA. (*Crossing down to table.*) Miss Alice going to be home to dinner tonight, Mrs. Sycamore? (*She puts pile of plates on table.*)

PENNY. (*Deep in her thinking.*) What? I don't know, Rheba. Maybe.

RHEBA. Well, I'll set a place for her, but she's only been home one night this week.

PENNY. Yes, I know.

RHEBA. (*She puts down a plate or two.*) Miss Essie's making some mighty good candy today. She's doing something new with cocoanuts. (*More plates.*)

PENNY. Uh-huh. That's nice.

RHEBA. Let's see . . . six and Mr. De Pinna, and if Mr. Kolenkhov comes that makes eight, don't it? (PENNY *types. At which point, a whistling sound of a rocket followed by a series of explosions comes up from cellar.* PENNY *and* RHEBA, *however, don't even notice it.* RHEBA *goes right on.*) Yes, I'd better set for eight. (*Puts napkins from chair to table. Puts down one more plate, looks over her setting of the table, and starts off* U.R.)

PENNY. (*Rising.*) Rheba, I think I'll put this play away for a while, and go back to the war play.

(ESSIE *returns from kitchen carrying a plate of freshly made candy.*)

RHEBA. Oh, I always liked that one—the war play. Boom, boom! (*She exits* U.R.)

ESSIE. (*Crossing over to* PENNY.) They'll be better when they're harder, Mother, but try one—I want to know what you think.

PENNY. Oh, they look lovely. (*She takes one.*) What do you call them?

ESSIE. I think I'll call 'em Love Dreams. (*She places them on* C. *table.*)

PENNY. Yes, that's nice. . . . (*Nibbling on one of the candies.*) I'm going back to my war play, Essie. What do you think?

ESSIE. (*Dances back to buffet.*) Oh, are you, Mother?

PENNY. (*Puts script down.*) Yes, I sort of got myself into a monastery and I can't get out.

ESSIE. (*Pointing her toe.*) Oh, well, it'll come to you, Mother. Remember how you got out of that brothel. . . . (*She looks at snake solarium, a glass structure looking something like a goldfish aquarium, but containing, believe it or not, snakes.*) The snakes look hungry. Did Rheba feed them?

(RHEBA *enters* U.R. *carrying silverware.*)

PENNY. (*As* RHEBA *re-enters, puts silverware down on table. Sets two places.*) I don't know. Rheba, did you feed the snakes yet?

RHEBA. No, Donald's coming and he always brings flies with him. (ESSIE *dances to* R. *of buffet.*)

PENNY. Well, try to feed them before Grandpa gets home. You know how fussy he is about them. (*Crossing to desk, she picks up file box with kittens in it.*)

RHEBA. (*Starts to go.*) Yes'm.

PENNY. (*Crossing to* RHEBA. *Handing her the kittens.*) And here, take Groucho and Harpo into the kitchen with you. (RHEBA *exits* U.R.) Believe I'll have another Love Dream. (*Sits at her desk.*)

(PAUL *emerges from cellar again.*)

PAUL. (*Enters* D.R. *and crosses to* ESSIE.) Mr. De Pinna was right about the balloon. It was too close to the powder.

ESSIE. (*Points to plate.*) Want a Love Dream, Father? They're on the table.

PAUL. (*Starts for stairs.*) No, thanks. I gotta wash.

PENNY. I'm going back to the war play, Paul.

PAUL. Oh, that's nice. We're putting some red stars after the bombs and *then* the balloon. That ought to do it. (*He goes up stairs.*)

ESSIE. (*Crossing down to back of chair* L. *of table.*) You know, Mr. Kolenkhov says I'm his most promising pupil.

PENNY. You'd think with forty monks and one girl that *some*thing would happen.

(ED CARMICHAEL *comes down stairs. A nondescript young man in his mid-thirties. He removes his coat as he crosses to xylophone.*)

ED. Essie! Heh! Essie! (PENNY *sits as music starts. He hums a snatch of melody as he heads for the far corner of the room—the xylophone corner. Arriving there, he picks up the sticks and continues the melody on the xylophone. Immediately* ESSIE *is up on her toes, performing intricate ballet steps to* ED'S *accompaniment.*)

ESSIE. (*After a bar, rising on toes—dancing—to* R. *below table.*) I like that, Ed. Did you write it? (PENNY *types.*)

ED. (*Pauses in his playing. Shakes his head.*) No, Beethoven. (*Music continues.*)

ESSIE. (*Never coming down off her toes.*) Lovely. Got a lot of *you* in it. . . . I made those new candies this afternoon, Ed. (*Dancing to the* L.) (PENNY *puts scripts from* U.S. *end to* D.S. *end.*)

ED. (*Playing away.*) Yah?

ESSIE. (*A series of leaping steps.*) You can take 'em around tonight.

ED. All right. . . . Now, here's the finish. This is me. (*He works up to an elaborate crescendo, but* ESSIE *keeps pace with him, right to the finish, pirouetting to the last note.*) How's that?

ESSIE. That's fine. (PENNY *picks up half of pile of scripts,* D.S. *end desk.*) Remember it when Kolenkhov comes, will you?

PENNY. (*Who has been busy with her scripts.*) Ed, dear. Why don't you and Essie have a baby? I was thinking about it just the other day.

(ED *puts xylophone hammers down—comes down from alcove.*)

ED. (*As* ESSIE *busies herself with her slippers.*) I don't know—we

10

could have one if you wanted us to. What about it, Essie? Do you want to have a baby?

ESSIE. Oh, I don't care. I'm willing if Grandpa is. (*And off into kitchen.*)

ED. (*Calling after her.*) Let's ask him.

PENNY. (*Running through a pile of scripts.*) Labor play, (ED *works printing press with a bang.*) religious play, (*Another bang.* RHEBA *enters* U.R. *with silverware. Puts table cover from chair on buffet arm.*) sex play— (*Still another bang.*) I know it's here some place.

DE PINNA. (*Coming out of cellar* D.R., *bound for kitchen to wash up.*) I was right about the balloon. It was too close to the powder.

ED. (*Who has crossed to his press.*) Anything you want printed, Mr. De Pinna? How about some more calling cards?

DE PINNA. No, thanks. I've still got the *first* thousand.

ED. Well, call on somebody, will you?

DE PINNA. All right! (*Exits* U.R.)

ED. (*Coming downstage—type stick in hand.*) What have we got for dinner, Rheba? I'm ready to print the menu.

RHEBA. Let's see. Corn flakes, watermelon, some of these candies Miss Essie made, and some kind of meat—I forget. (*Sets silverware.*)

ED. I think I'll set it up in bold face Cheltenham tonight. (*Going to printing press* U.R.) You know, if I'm going to take those new candies around I'd better print up some descriptive matter after dinner.

PENNY. Do you think anybody reads those things, Ed—that you put in the candy boxes? . . . Oh, here's the war play. (*She pulls a script out of pile.*) "Poison Gas." (*The doorbell rings. Changes tone.*) I guess that's Donald. (RHEBA *smiles and starts for hall door,* U.L.) Look at Rheba smile.

ED. The boy friend, eh, Rheba?

(RHEBA *is out of sight.*)

PENNY. They're awfully cute, Donald and Rheba. Sort of like Porgy and Bess.

DONALD. (Off stage.) Hello, Rheba.

RHEBA. Donald! (RHEBA *having opened door,* DONALD *now looms up in arch, straw hat in hand.*)

DONALD. Evening, everybody!

ED. Hi, Donald! How've you been?

11

DONALD. (*Coming into room.*) I'm pretty good, Mr. Ed. How you been, Mrs. Sycamore. (*He starts* R.)

PENNY. Very well, thank you. (*Rises.*) Donald?

DONALD. Yes, ma'am?

PENNY. Were you ever in a monastery?

DONALD. No-o. I don't go no place much. I'm on relief. (*Reaching for bottle of flies in his pocket.*)

PENNY. Ah, yes, of course. (*Sits.*)

DONALD. (*Crossing to* RHEBA. *Pulling a bottle out of side pocket.*) Here's the flies, Rheba. Caught a big mess of them today.

RHEBA. (*Taking the jar.*) You sure did. (RHEBA *goes into the kitchen* U.R.) (DONALD *crosses to* L.)

DONALD. I see you've been working, Mrs. Sycamore.

PENNY. Yes, indeed, Donald.

DONALD. How's Grandpa?

PENNY. Just fine. He's over at Columbia this afternoon. The Commencement exercises.

DONALD. (*Crossing to table.*) My . . . my. The years certainly do roll 'round. M-m-m. (*Takes a candy.*)

ED. (*With his typesetting.*) M—E—A—T. . . . What's he go there for all the time, Penny?

PENNY. I don't know, it's so handy—just around the corner.

(PAUL *comes down stairs, an impressive looking tome under his arm.*)

PAUL. Oh, Donald! Mr. De Pinna and I are going to take the fireworks up to Mount Vernon next week. Do you think you could give us a hand?

DONALD. Yes, sir, only I can't take no money for it this year, because if the Government finds out I'm working they'll get sore.

PAUL. Oh! (DONALD *drifts up to buffet and feeds bits of candy to the snakes.*) Ed, I got a wonderful idea in the bathroom just now. I was reading Trotzky. It's yours, isn't it?

ED. (*Crossing down.*) Yah, I left it there.

PENNY. *Who* is it?

PAUL. (*A step to* PENNY.) You know, Trotzky. The Russian Revolution. (*Showing her book.*)

PENNY. Oh.

PAUL. (DONALD *turns.*) Anyhow, it struck me it was a great fireworks idea. Remember "The Last Days of Pompeii"?

PENNY. Oh, yes. Palisades Park. (*With a gesture of her arms she loosely describes a couple of arcs, indicative of the eruption of Mt. Vesuvius.*) That's where we met.

PAUL. Well, I'm going to do the Revolution! A full hour display.

DONALD. Say!

PENNY. Paul, that's wonderful!

ED. The red fire is the flag, huh?

PAUL. (*Crossing a step to* R.) Sure! And the Czar, and the Cossacks!

DONALD. And the freeing of the slaves?

PAUL. No, no, Donald—the Russian Revolution. (*The sound of the front door slamming. A second's pause, then* GRANDPA *enters living room.* GRANDPA *is about 75, a wiry little man whom the years have treated kindly. His face is youthful, despite the lines that sear it; his eyes are very much alive. He is a man who made his peace with the world long, long ago, and his whole attitude and manner are quietly persuasive of this.*) Hello, Grandpa. (DONALD *crosses to door* U.R. ED *up to* L. *of xylophone.* PAUL *sits above table.*)

GRANDPA. (*Putting his hat on newel post and surveying the group.*) Well, sir, you should have been there. That's all I can say—you should have been there.

PENNY. Was it a nice Commencement, Grandpa?

GRANDPA. Wonderful. They get better every year. (*He peers into snake solarium.*) You don't know how lucky you are you're snakes. (*Crossing to alcove for his house coat.*)

ED. Big class this year, Grandpa? How many were there?

GRANDPA. Oh, must have been two acres. *Everybody* graduated. (*Removes street coat.*) Yes, sir. And much funnier speeches than they had last year. (*Crossing down to his chair, putting on house coat.*)

DONALD. (*Coming* D.S.) You want to listen to a good speech you go up and hear Father Divine.

GRANDPA. I'll wait—they'll have him at Columbia. (*Sits* R. *of table, as* DONALD *crosses to* R.)

PENNY. Donald, will you tell Rheba Grandpa's home now and we won't wait for Miss Alice.

(DE PINNA *enters from kitchen, rolling down his sleeves.*)

DONALD. Yes'm . . . (*As he exits through kitchen door* U.R.) Rheba, Grandpa's home . . . we can have dinner.

PAUL. We made a new skyrocket today, Grandpa. Wait till you see it.

DE PINNA. Evening, Grandpa.

13

GRANDPA. (*Starting to remove his shoes.*) Evening, Mr. De Pinna.

PAUL. Didn't we make a fine rocket today, Mr. De Pinna?

DE PINNA. (*As he exits through cellar door* D.R.) We certainly did.

PAUL. Wonder why they don't have fireworks at Commencements?

GRANDPA. Don't make enough noise. You take a good Commencement orator and he'll drown out a whole carload of fireworks. (ED *gets a new pair of hammers.*) And say just as much, too.

PENNY. Don't the graduates ever say anything?

GRANDPA. No, they just sit there in cap and nightgown, get their diplomas, and then along about forty years from now they suddenly say, "Where am I?"

ESSIE. (ESSIE *enters from kitchen, carrying a plate of tomatoes for the evening meal.*) Hello, Grandpa. Have a nice day?

GRANDPA. Hello-have-a-nice-day. Don't I even get kissed?

ESSIE. (*Kissing him.*) Excuse me, Grandpa.

GRANDPA. I'll take a tomato, too. (ED *strikes three tentative notes on xylophone.* GRANDPA *takes a tomato and sits with it in his hand, weighing it.*) You know I could have used a couple of these this afternoon. . . .

ESSIE. (*Offering plate to* PAUL.) Father?

(*Again* ED *strikes the keys of his xylophone.*)

PAUL. No, thanks.

(ESSIE *crosses to* PENNY.)

ESSIE. Mother?

PENNY. No, thanks, dear.

GRANDPA. Play something, Ed.

ED. All right. (ED *at once obliges on the xylophone. Immediately* ESSIE *is up on her toes, drifting through the mazes of a toe dance, placing plate of tomatoes on the table as she dances.*)

ESSIE. (*After a moment of dancing "The Dying Swan."*) There was a letter came for you, Grandpa. Did you get it?

GRANDPA. (*Cutting a tomato.*) Letter for me? I don't know anybody.

ESSIE. It was for you, though. Had your name on it.

GRANDPA. That's funny. Where is it?

ESSIE. I don't know. Where's Grandpa's letter, Mother?

PENNY. (*Who has been deep in her work.*) What, dear?

ESSIE. (*Dancing dreamily away.*) Where's that letter that came for Grandpa last week?

14

PENNY. I don't know. (*Then brightly.*) I remember seeing the kittens on it. (ESSIE *starts to floor.*)

GRANDPA. Who was it from? Did you notice?

ESSIE. Yes, it was on the outside.

GRANDPA. Well, who was it?

ESSIE. (*First finishing the graceful flutterings of "The Dying Swan."*) United States Government. (*The music ends.*)

GRANDPA. Really? Wonder what *they* wanted.

ESSIE. (*Rising and starting* R.) There was one before that, too, from the same people. There was a couple of them.

GRANDPA. Well, if any more come I wish you'd give them to me.

ESSIE. (*Exits through kitchen door on her toes.*) Yes, Grandpa.

GRANDPA. (*Rises—shoes in hand.*) I think I'll go out to Westchester tomorrow and do a little snake-hunting. (*Starts up to alcove for slippers.*) (ED *looks over xylophone, figuring out tune.*)

PAUL. (*Who has settled down with his book some time before this.*) "God is the State; the State is God."

GRANDPA. What's that? (*Coming down—slippers in one hand, album in the other.*)

PAUL. "God is the State; the State is God."

GRANDPA. Who says that?

PAUL. Trotsky.

GRANDPA. Well, that's all right—I thought *you* said it. (*Sits* R. *of table.*)

ED. It's nice for printing, you know. Good and short. (*He reaches into type case.*) G—O—D—space—I—S—space—T—H—E—space ——

(*The sound of the outer door closing, and* ALICE SYCAMORE *enters the room. A lovely, fresh young girl of about twenty-two. She is plainly* GRANDPA'S *granddaughter, but there is something that sets her apart from the rest of the family. For one thing, she is in daily contact with the world; in addition, she seems to have escaped the tinge of mild insanity that pervades the rest of them. But she is a Sycamore for all that, and her devotion and love for them are plainly apparent. At the moment she is in a small, nervous flutter, but she is doing her best to conceal it.*)

ALICE. (*As she makes the rounds, kissing her mother, her father, her grandfather.*) And so the beautiful princess came into the palace, and kissed her mother, and her father, and her grandfather ——

GRANDPA. Hello, darling!

ALICE. Hi, Grandpa—and what do you think? They turned into the Sycamore family. Surprised? (*Removing her hat.*) (ED *gets another set of hammers.*)

ESSIE. (*Enters* U.R. *Examining* ALICE'S *dress.*) Oh, Alice, I like it.

ALICE. Do you?

ESSIE. It's new, isn't it?

PENNY. Looks nice and summery.

ESSIE. Where'd you get it?

ALICE. Oh, I took a walk during lunch hour.

GRANDPA. You've been taking a lot of walks lately. That's the second new dress this week.

ALICE. (*Takes off gloves.*) I just like to brighten up the office once in a while. I'm known as the Kay Francis of Kirby & Co. . . . Well, what's new around here? In the way of plays, snakes, ballet dancing or fireworks. Dad, I'll bet you've been down in that cellar all day. (ED *sees if hammers are straight.*)

PAUL. Huh?

PENNY. I'm going back to the war play, Alice. (ESSIE *does dance step exercise.*)

ALICE. Really, Mother? (*She takes her hat to the hatrack.*) (ED *strikes a note on xylophone.*)

ESSIE. Ed, play Alice that Beethoven thing you wrote.

(ED *at xylophone. He plays.* ESSIE *is up on her toes.*)

GRANDPA. You know, you can mail a letter all the way from Nicaragua now for two pesetos.

PAUL. Really?

PENNY. (*Reading from her script.*) "Kenneth! My virginity is a priceless thing to me."

ALICE. Listen, people. . . . Listen. (*The music dies out. She gets a scattered sort of attention.*) I'm not home to dinner. A young gentleman is calling for me. (ED *fixes a xylophone hammer.*)

ESSIE. Really, who is it?

PENNY. Well, isn't that nice?

ALICE. I did everything possible to keep him from coming here but he's calling for me.

PENNY. Why don't you both stay to dinner?

ALICE. No, I want him to take you in easy doses. I've tried to prepare him a little, but don't make it any worse than you can help. Don't read him any plays, Mother, and don't let a snake bite him,

16

Grandpa, because I like him. And I wouldn't dance for him, Essie, because we're going to the Monte Carlo ballet tonight.

GRANDPA. Can't do *anything*. Who *is* he—President of the United States?

ALICE. (*Crossing to* L. *of* C. *table.*) No, he's vice-president of Kirby & Co. Mr. Anthony Kirby, Jr.

ESSIE. The boss's son?

PENNY. Well!

ALICE. (*A step to* PENNY.) The boss's son. Just like the movies.

ESSIE. (*Crossing down.*) That explains the new dresses.

ED. (*Comes down a step.*) And not being home to dinner for three weeks.

ALICE. Why, Sherlock Holmes!

PENNY. (*Rises. All aglow, script in hand.*) Are you going to marry him?

ALICE. Oh, of course. Tonight! Meanwhile I have to go up and put on my wedding dress. (PENNY *laughs, crosses to desk.*)

ESSIE. Is he good-looking?

ALICE. (*Vainly consulting her watch. Starts* U.S.) Yes, in a word . . . Oh, dear! What time is it?

PENNY. (*Preoccupied with scripts.*) I don't know. Anybody know what time it is?

PAUL. Mr. De Pinna might know.

ED. It was about five o'clock a couple of hours ago.

ALICE. Oh, I ought to know better than to ask you people. . . . Will you let me know the minute he comes, please?

PENNY. Of course, Alice.

ALICE. Yes, I know, but I mean the *minute* he comes.

PENNY. Why, of course.

(ALICE *looks apprehensively from one to the other; then disappears up the stairs* U.L.)

ALICE. Well, be sure.

PENNY. Well, what do you think of that?

GRANDPA. She seems to like him, if you ask me.

ESSIE. I should say so. She's got it bad.

(ED *crosses into the room.*)

PENNY. (*Crossing to* R. *a bit.*) Wouldn't it be wonderful if she married him? We could have the wedding right in this room.

PAUL. Now, wait a minute, Penny. This is the first time he's ever called for the girl.

(ESSIE *stretching exercise.*)

PENNY. You only called for me once.

PAUL. Young people are different nowadays.

ESSIE. Oh, I don't know. Look at Ed and me. He came to dinner *once* and just stayed. (*Toe pointing.*)

PENNY. Anyhow, I think it's wonderful. Don't you, Grandpa?

GRANDPA. She certainly seems happy about it.

PENNY. He must be crazy about her. Maybe he's the one who is taking her out every night. (*Door bell.*) There he is! Never mind, Rheba, I'll answer it. (*She is fluttering to the door.*) Now remember what Alice said, and be *very* nice to him.

GRANDPA. (*Rising.*) All right—let's take a look at him.

(PAUL *rises,* ED *puts on his coat and comes into room. They all stand awaiting the stranger's appearance.*)

PENNY. (*At the front door; milk and honey in her voice.*) Well! Welcome to our little home!

HENDERSON. How do you do?

PENNY. I'm Alice's mother. Do come right in! Here we are! (*She reappears in archway, piloting the stranger, holding his hand.*) This is Grandpa, and that's Alice's father, and Alice's sister and her husband, Ed Carmichael. (*The family all give courteous little nods and smiles as they are introduced.*) Well! Now give me your hat and make yourself right at home. (PENNY *takes his hat.*)

THE MAN. I'm afraid you must be making a mistake. (*Reaching for his card.*)

PENNY. How's that?

THE MAN. My card.

PENNY. (*Reading.*) "Wilbur C. Henderson. Internal Revenue Department."

(PAUL *and* GRANDPA *exchange looks.*)

HENDERSON. That's right.

GRANDPA. What can we do for you?

HENDERSON. Does a Mr. Martin Vanderhof live here?

GRANDPA. Yes, sir. That's me.

HENDERSON. (*Coming down to table.*) Well, Mr. Vanderhof, the Government wants to talk to you about a little matter of income tax.

PENNY. Income tax?

HENDERSON. You mind if I sit down?

GRANDPA. No, no. Just go right ahead.

HENDERSON. (*Settling himself in a chair* L. *of the table.*) Thank you. (GRANDPA *sits. From above stairs the voice of* ALICE *floats down.*)

ALICE. Mother! Is that Mr. Kirby?

PENNY. (*Going to stairs.*) No. No, it isn't, darling. It's—an internal something or other. (*To* HENDERSON.) Pardon me.

DE PINNA. (*Entering from* D.R. *carrying a firecracker.*) Mr. Sycamore . . . oh, excuse me.

PAUL. What is it?

DE PINNA. (*Crossing to* PAUL.) These things are not going off. Look. (*He strikes a match.*)

PAUL. Not here, Mr. De Pinna. Grandpa's busy.

DE PINNA. Oh!

(*They start for hall.*)

PAUL. Pardon me.

(*They start again for hall,* DE PINNA *looking at* HENDERSON *until* PAUL *and* DE PINNA *exit.*)

HENDERSON. (*Pulling a sheaf of papers from his pocket.*) Now, Mr. Vanderhof, (*A quick look toward hall.*) we've written you several letters about this, but have not had any reply. (PENNY *sits in her desk chair.*)

GRANDPA. Oh, that's what those letters were.

ESSIE. (*Sitting on couch* R.) I told you they were from the Government.

HEND. According to our records, Mr. Vanderhof, you have never paid an income tax.

GRANDPA. That's right.

HEND. Why not?

GRANDPA. I don't believe in it.

HEND. Well—you own property, don't you?

GRANDPA. Yes, sir.

HEND. And you receive a yearly income from it?

GRANDPA. I do.

HEND. Of—(*He consults his records.*)—between three and four thousand dollars.

GRANDPA. About that.

HEND. You've been receiving it for years.

GRANDPA. I have. 1901, if you want the exact date.

HEND. Well, the Government is only concerned from 1914 on. That's when the income tax started. (*Pause.*)

GRANDPA. Well?

HEND. Well—it seems, Mr. Vanderhof, that you owe the Government twenty-four years' back income tax.

ED. (*Coming down as* ESSIE *joins him.*) Wait a minute! You can't go back that far—that's outlawed.

HEND. (*Calmly regarding him.*) M-m-m! What's *your* name?

ED. What difference does that make?

HEND. Ever file an income tax return?

ED. (*Turns to* ESSIE, ESSIE *steps in.*) No, sir.

HEND. Ah! What was your income last year?

ED. Ah—twenty-eight dollars and fifty cents, wasn't it, Essie?

ESSIE. Yes, sir.

HEND. If you please! (*Dismissing* ED *and* ESSIE. *They drift* U.S.) Now, Mr. Vanderhof, you know there's quite a penalty for not filing an income tax return.

PENNY. Penalty?

GRANDPA. Look, Mr. Henderson, let me ask you something.

HEND. Well?

GRANDPA. Suppose I pay you this money—mind you, I don't say I'm going to pay it—but just for the sake of argument—what's the Government going to do with it?

HEND. How do you mean?

GRANDPA. Well, what do I get for my money? If I go into Macy's and buy something, there it *is*—I see it. What's the Government give me?

HEND. Why, the Government gives you everything. It protects you.

GRANDPA. What from?

HEND. Well—invasion. Foreigners that might come over here and take everything you've got.

GRANDPA. Oh, I don't think they're going to do that.

HEND. If you didn't pay an income tax, they would. How do you think the Government keeps up the Army and Navy? All those battleships . . .

GRANDPA. Last time we used battleships was in the Spanish-American War, and what did we get out of it? Cuba—and we gave that back. I wouldn't mind paying if it were something sensible.

HEND. Sensible? Well, what about Congress, and the Supreme Court, and the President? We've got to pay *them,* don't we?

GRANDPA. Not with my money—no, sir.

HEND. (*Furious. Rises, picks up papers.*) Now wait a minute! I'm not here to argue with you. (*Crossing* L.) All I know is that you haven't paid an income tax and you've got to pay it!

GRANDPA. They've got to show me.

HEND. (*Yelling.*) We *don't* have to show you! I just told you! All those buildings down in Washington, (*To* PENNY. *She nods.*) and Interstate Commerce, and the Constitution!

GRANDPA. The Constitution was paid for long ago. And Interstate Commerce—what *is* Interstate Commerce, anyhow?

HEND. (*Business of look at* PENNY—*at* ED—*at* GRANDPA. *With murderous calm, crosses and places his hands on table.*) There are forty-eight states—see? And if there weren't Interstate Commerce, nothing could go from one state to another. See?

GRANDPA. Why not? They got fences?

HEND. (*To* GRANDPA.) No, they haven't got fences. They've got *laws!* (*Crossing up to arch* L.) My God, I never came across anything like *this* before!

GRANDPA. Well, I might pay about seventy-five dollars, but that's all it's worth.

HEND. You'll pay every cent of it, like everybody else!

ED. (*Who has lost interest.*) Listen, Essie—listen to this a minute.

(*The xylophone again;* ESSIE *goes into her dance.*)

HEND. (*Going right ahead, battling against the music.*) And let me tell you something else! You'll go to jail (PENNY *rises.*) if you don't pay, do you hear that? That's the law, and if you think you're bigger than the law, you've got another think coming. You're no better than anybody else, and the sooner you get that through your head, the better . . . you'll hear from the United States Government, that's all I can say. . . . (*The music has stopped. He is backing out of the room.*)

GRANDPA. (*Quietly.*) Look out for those snakes.

HEND. (*Jumping; exits off* L.) Jesus! (*An explosion from the hall. He exits through hall door.*)

ED. How was that, Essie?

ESSIE. Fine, Ed.

PAUL. (*Entering from hall with* DE PINNA.) How did that sound to you folks? (ESSIE *sits on couch.*)

21

GRANDPA. I liked it.

PENNY. My goodness, he was mad, wasn't he?

GRANDPA. It's not his fault. It's just that the whole thing is so silly.

PENNY. He forgot his hat.

GRANDPA. Say, what size is that hat?

PENNY. Seven and an eighth.

GRANDPA. Just right for me.

DE PINNA. Who was that fellow, anyway? (*Door bell. As bell rings* DE PINNA *makes for cellar door to get his coat.*)

PENNY. This *must* be Mr. Kirby.

PAUL. Better make sure this time.

PENNY. Yes, I will. (*She disappears* U.L.)

ESSIE. (*Rises.*) I hope he's good-looking.

(*The family is again standing awaiting the newcomer.*)

PENNY. (*Heard at the door.*) How do you do?

MAN'S VOICE. Good evening.

PENNY. (*Taking no chances.*) Is this Mr. Anthony Kirby, Jr.?

TONY. (*Business.* PAUL *affirms it.* ED *and* ESSIE *come* D.S.) Yes. (GRANDPA *rises.*)

PENNY. (*Giving her all.*) Well, Mr. Kirby, come right in! We've been expecting you. Come right in! (*They come into sight;* PENNY *expansively addresses the family.*) This is *really* Mr. Kirby! Now, I'm Alice's mother, and that's *Mr.* Sycamore, and Alice's grandfather, and her sister Essie, and Essie's husband. (DE PINNA *waves for recognition. There are a few mumbled greetings.*) There! Now you know *all* of us, Mr. Kirby. Give me your hat and make yourself right at home.

(TONY KIRBY *comes a few steps into the room. He is a personable young man, not long out of Yale, and, as we will presently learn, even more recently out of Cambridge. Although he fits all the physical requirements of a boss's son, his face has something of the idealist in it. All in all, a very nice young man.*)

TONY. Thank you.

(*Again the voice of the vigilant* ALICE *floats down from upstairs.* "Is that Mr. Kirby, Mother?")

PENNY. (*Shouting up stairs.*) Yes, Alice. It is. He's *lovely!*

ALICE. (*Aware of storm signals.*) I'll be right down.

PENNY. (*Puts* TONY'S *hat on desk.*) Do sit down, Mr. Kirby.

TONY. (PAUL *places* TONY'S *chair.*) Thank you. (*A glance at dinner table.*) I hope I'm not keeping you from dinner?

GRANDPA. No, no. Have a tomato? (*He sits. Also* PAUL.)

TONY. No, thank you.

PENNY. (*Producing candy-filled skull, crosses to* TONY.) How about a piece of candy?

TONY. (*Eyeing the container.*) Ah—no, thanks. (DE PINNA *again steps forward.*)

PENNY. Oh, I forgot to introduce Mr. De Pinna. This is Mr. De Pinna, Mr. Kirby. (*An exchange of "How do you do's?"*)

DE PINNA. Wasn't I reading about your father in the newspaper the other day? Didn't he get indicted or something?

TONY. (*Smiling.*) Hardly that. He just testified before the Securities Commission.

DE PINNA. Oh.

PENNY. (*Sharply.*) Yes, of course. I'm sure there was nothing crooked about it, Mr. De Pinna. As a matter of fact—(*She is now addressing* TONY. *Drawing forward her desk chair, she sits.*)—Alice has often told us what a lovely man your father is.

TONY. (*Sitting* L. *of table.*) Well, I know Father couldn't get along without Alice. She knows more about the business than any of us.

ESSIE. You're awful young Mr. Kirby, aren't you, to be vice-president of a big place like that?

TONY. Well, you know what that means, vice-president. All I have is a desk with my name on it.

PENNY. Is that all? Don't you get any salary?

TONY. (*With a laugh.*) Well, a little. More than I'm worth, I'm afraid. (DE PINNA *lights pipe.*)

PENNY. Now you're just being modest.

GRANDPA. Sounds kind of dull to me—Wall Street. Do you like it?

TONY. Well, the hours are short. And I haven't been there very long.

GRANDPA. Just out of college, huh?

TONY. Well, I knocked around for a while first. Just sort of had fun.

GRANDPA. What did you do? Travel?

TONY. For a while. Then I went to Cambridge for a year.

GRANDPA. (*Nodding.*) England.

TONY. That's right.

GRANDPA. Say, what's an English commencement like? Did you see any?

23

TONY. Oh, very impressive.

GRANDPA. They are, huh?

TONY. Anyhow, now the fun's over, and—I'm facing the world.

PENNY. Well, you've certainly got a good start, Mr. Kirby. Vice-president, and a rich father.

TONY. Well, that's hardly my fault.

PENNY. (*Brightly.*) So now I suppose you're all ready to settle down and—get married.

PAUL. Come now, Penny, I'm sure Mr. Kirby knows his own mind.

PENNY. I wasn't making up his mind for him—was I, Mr. Kirby?

TONY. That's quite all right, Mrs. Sycamore.

PENNY. (*To the others.*) You see?

ESSIE. You mustn't rush him, Mother.

PENNY. Well, all I meant was he's bound to get married, (ALICE *starts down stairs.*) and suppose the wrong girl gets him?

(*The descending* ALICE *mercifully comes to* TONY'S *rescue at this moment. Her voice is heard from stairs.* TONY *rises.*)

ALICE. Well, here I am, a vision in blue. (*She comes into the room —and very lovely indeed.*) Apparently you've had time to get acquainted. (ESSIE *a step upstage.* TONY *rises. Also* PAUL.)

PENNY. (*Rises and pushes chair back.*) Oh, yes, indeed. We were just having a delightful talk about love and marriage.

ALICE. Oh, dear. (*She turns to* TONY. RHEBA *enters.*) I'm sorry. I came down as fast as I could.

TONY. I didn't mind in the least.

RHEBA. (*Enters* U.R. *bringing a platter of sliced watermelon.*) Damn those flies in the kitchen. (ALICE *looks at* PENNY *and back to* TONY.) Oh, Miss Alice, you look beautiful. Where you going?

ALICE. (*Making the best of it.*) I'm going out, Rheba.

RHEBA. (*Noticing* TONY—*looks at him.*) Stepping, huh?

(*The door bell sounds.* RHEBA *puts platter on table and crosses to hall door.*)

ESSIE. That must be Kolenkhov.

ALICE. (*Uneasily. She crosses to* U.L.) I think we'd better go, Tony.

TONY. (*Crossing to desk.*) All right.

(*Before they can escape, however,* DONALD *emerges from kitchen* U.R. *bearing a tray.*)

DONALD. Grandpa, you take cream on your corn flakes? I forget.

GRANDPA. Half and half, Donald.

(DONALD *exits* U.R. *The voice of* BORIS KOLENKHOV *booms from outer door.*)

KOLENKHOV. Ah, my little Rhebishka!
GRANDPA. Yes, that's Kolenkhov, all right.
RHEBA. (*With a scream of laughter.*) Yessuh, Mr. Kolenkhov!
KOL. Good evening, everybody!
ALL. Good evening.

(*He appears in archway, his great arm completely encircling the delighted* RHEBA. MR. KOLENKHOV *is one of* RHEBA'S *pets, and if you like Russians he might be one of yours. He is enormous, hairy, loud, and very, very Russian. His appearance in the archway still further traps* ALICE *and* TONY. RHEBA *exits* U.R.)

KOL. (*As he comes* D.S.) Grandpa, what do you think? I have had a letter from Russia! The Second Five-Year Plan is a failure! (*Throws hat on buffet. He lets out a laugh that shakes the rafters.*)
ESSIE. I practiced today, Mr. Kolenkhov!
KOL. (*With a deep Russian bow and a click of heels.*) My Pavlowa!
ALICE. (*Crossing down.*) Well, if you'll excuse us, Mr. Kolenkhov. (PENNY *hands* TONY *his hat.*)
KOL. My little Alice! (*He kisses her hand.*) Never have I seen you look so magnificent.
ALICE. Thank you, Mr. Kolenkhov. (KOLENKHOV *steps back.*) Tony, this is Mr. Kolenkhov, Essie's dancing teacher. Mr. Kirby.
TONY. How do you do?
KOL. How do you do? (*A click of the heels and a bow from* KOLENKHOV.)
ALICE. (*Determined, this time. A step down.*) Will you pardon us, Mr. Kolenkhov—we're going to the Monte Carlo Ballet.
KOL. (*At the top of his tremendous voice.*) The Monte Carlo Ballet! It *stinks.* (*Crossing* U.C.)
ALICE. (*Panicky now.*) Yes. . . . Well—good-bye, everybody. Good-bye.
TONY. Good-bye. I'm so glad to have met you all.

(*A chorus of answering "Good-byes" from the family. The young people are gone. The sound of hall door closing.*)

DE PINNA. Good-bye.

KOL. (*Still furious, crosses* L.) Monte Carlo Ballet!

PENNY. Isn't Mr. Kirby lovely? . . . Come on, everybody! Dinner's ready! (PAUL *indicates chair.*)

ED. (*Pulling up chair from alcove.*) I thought he was a nice fellow, didn't you? (*Gets another chair from hall.*)

ESSIE. (*Doing her toe steps.*) Mm. (*Bending.*) And so good-looking.

PENNY. And he had such nice manners. Did you notice, Paul? Did you notice his manners?

PAUL. I certainly did. You were getting pretty personal with him.

PENNY. Oh, now, Paul. . . . Anyhow, he's a very nice young man. (DE PINNA *brings chair from alcove.*)

DE PINNA. (*As he seats himself.*) He looks like a cousin of mine. (ESSIE *bends.*)

KOL. Bakst! Diaghileff! *Then* you had the *ballet!*

PENNY. I think if they get married here I'll put the altar right where the snakes are. You wouldn't mind, Grandpa, would you?

GRANDPA. Not if the snakes don't.

ESSIE. (*Crossing to chair back of table and sitting.*) Oh, no, they'll want to get married in a church. His family and everything.

DE PINNA. I like a church wedding.
ED. Yes, of course they would.   } (*Together.*)
KOL. Of course.

GRANDPA. (*Tapping on a plate for silence.*) Quiet, everybody! Quiet! (*They are immediately silent. . . . Grace is about to be pronounced.* GRANDPA *pauses a moment for her to bow then raises his eyes heavenward. He clears his throat and proceeds to say Grace.*) Well, Sir, we've been getting along pretty good for quite a while now, and we're certainly much obliged. Remember, all we ask is to just go along and be happy in our own sort of way. Of course we want to keep our health but as far as anything else is concerned, we'll leave it to You. Thank You. (RHEBA *to* KOLENKHOV. *The heads come up as* RHEBA *and* DONALD *enter through kitchen door with steaming platters.*) So the Second Five-Year Plan is a failure, eh, Kolenkhov?

KOL. Catastrophic! And wait until they try the Third Five-Year Plan!

PENNY. (*On the cue "Thank You."*) Of course his family is going to want to come. Imagine. Alice marrying a Kirby!

ESSIE. Think of that. Isn't it exciting?

26

ED. I'll play the wedding march on the xylophone.

PAUL. What have we got for dinner? I'm hungry.

CURTAIN

ACT I

SCENE 2: *Late the same night. The house is in darkness save for a light in the hall. An accordion is heard off stage* R., *then suddenly a good loud BANG! from the cellar. Somewhere in the nether regions, one of the Sycamores is still at work.*

As the accordion player finishes the song the sound of a key in the outer door. The voices of ALICE *and* TONY *drift through.*

ALICE. (*Off stage.*) I could see them dance every night of the week. I think they're marvelous.

TONY. They are, aren't they? But of course just walking inside any theatre gives *me* a thrill.

ALICE. (*As they come into sight in hallway.*) Well, it's been *so* lovely, Tony, I hate to have it over.

TONY. Oh, is it over? Do I have to go right away?

ALICE. Not if you don't want to.

TONY. I don't.

ALICE. Would you like a cold drink?

TONY. Wonderful. (ALICE *pauses to switch on lights.*)

ALICE. I'll see what's in the icebox. Want to come along?

TONY. I'd follow you to the ends of the earth.

ALICE. (*At door.*) Oh just the kitchen is enough.

(*They exit through kitchen door. A pause, and the lights go on.*)

TONY. Why, I like it. You've done it very simply, haven't you?

ALICE. Yes, we didn't know whether to do it Empire or Neo-Grecian.

TONY. So you settled for Frigidaire.

ALICE. Yes, it's so easy to live with. (*They return.* ALICE *crosses to table. She is carrying two glasses.* TONY, *a bottle of ginger ale and a bottle opener.*) Lucky you're not hungry, Mr. K. An icebox full of corn flakes. That gives you a rough idea of the Sycamores. (TONY *follows down to table.*)

TONY. (*Working away with the opener.*) Of course, why they make these bottle openers for Singer midgets I never did . . . (*As bottle opens.*) All over my coat.

ALICE. (*As she hands him a glass.*) I'll take mine in a glass, if you don't mind.

TONY. (*Pouring.*) There you are. A foaming beaker. (*Pours his own.*)

ALICE. Anyhow, it's cold.

TONY. (*As* ALICE *sits* R. *of the table.*) Now if you'll please be seated, I'd like to offer a toast.

ALICE. We are seated.

TONY. Miss Sycamore (*He raises his glass on high.*) . . . to you.

ALICE. Thank you, Mr. Kirby. (*Lifting her own glass.*) To you. (*She drinks and puts glass down.*)

TONY. You know something?

ALICE. What?

TONY. (*Puts his glass down and sighs happily.*) I wouldn't trade one minute of this evening for . . . all the rice in China.

ALICE. Really?

TONY. Cross my heart.

ALICE. (*A little sigh of contentment. Then shyly.*) Is there much rice in China?

TONY. Terrific. Didn't you read "The Good Earth"? (*She laughs. They are silent for a moment. He sighs and looks at his watch.*) Well, I suppose I ought to go.

ALICE. Is it very late?

TONY. (*Looks at his watch.*) Very. (ALICE *gives a little nod. Time doesn't matter.*) I don't want to go.

ALICE. I don't want you to.

TONY. All right, I won't. (*Sits* L. *of table. Silence again.*) When do you get your vacation?

ALICE. Last two weeks in August.

TONY. I might take mine then, too.

ALICE. Really?

TONY. What are you going to do?

ALICE. I don't know. I hadn't thought much about it.

TONY. Going away, do you think?

ALICE. I might not. I like the city in the summer time.

TONY. I do too.

ALICE. But you always go up to Maine, don't you?

TONY. That's right. (*Rises.*) Oh—but I'm sure I *would* like the city in the summer time, if —— Oh, you know what I mean, Alice. I'd love it if *you* were here.

ALICE. Well—it'd be nice if you were here, Tony. (*Rises and crosses to* R.)

TONY. You know what you're saying, don't you?

ALICE. What?

TONY. That you'd rather spend the summer with me than anybody else.

ALICE. (*Back to* TONY.) Was I?

TONY. (*Crossing few steps* R.) Well, if it's true about the summer, how would you feel about—the winter?

ALICE. (*Seeming to weigh the matter. Turns to* TONY.) Yes, I'd—like that too.

TONY. (*Tremulous.*) Then there's spring and autumn. If you could —see your way clear about those, Miss Sycamore? (*Crossing to* ALICE.)

ALICE. (*Again a little pause.*) I might.

TONY. I guess that's the whole year. We haven't forgotten anything, have we?

ALICE. No.

TONY. Well, then —— (*Another pause; their eyes meet.* TONY *starts to embrace* ALICE. *And at this moment,* PENNY *is heard from stairway.* TONY *crosses to back of* GRANDPA'S *chair.*)

PENNY. (*Off stage.*) Is that you, Alice? What time is it? (*She comes into room, wrapped in a bathrobe.*) Oh! (*In sudden embarrassment.*) Excuse me, Mr. Kirby. I had no idea—that is, I—(*She senses the situation.*) —I didn't mean to interrupt anything.

TONY. Not at all, Mrs. Sycamore.

ALICE. (*Quietly.*) No, Mother.

PENNY. I just came down for a manuscript—(*Fumbling at her desk.*)—then you can go right ahead. Ah, here it is. "Sex Takes a Holiday." Well—good night, Tony.

TONY. Good night, Mrs. Sycamore.

PENNY. Oh, I think you can call me Penny, don't you, Alice? At least I hope so. (*With a little laugh she vanishes up stairs.*) (TONY *turns back to* ALICE. *Before* PENNY'S *rippling laugh quite dies,* BANG! *from the cellar.* TONY *jumps.*)

TONY. What's that?

ALICE. (*Quietly. She crosses to below table.*) It's all right, Tony. That's father.

TONY. Oh—this time of night? (*Coming* D.S.)

29

ALICE. (*Ominously—turns to* TONY.) *Any* time of night. Any time of *day*. (*She stands silent.*) (*In the pause,* TONY *gazes at her fondly.*)

TONY. (*Crossing to* ALICE.) You know, you're more beautiful, more lovely, more adorable than anyone else in the whole world.

ALICE. (*As he starts to embrace her, she backs away.*) Don't, Tony.

TONY. What? (*As* ALICE *shakes her head.*) My dear, just because your mother . . . all mothers are like that, Alice, and Penny's a darling. You see I'm even calling her Penny.

ALICE. I don't mean that. (*She faces him squarely—crosses to* TONY.) Look, Tony, this is something I should have said a long time ago, but I didn't have the courage. (*Turns away.*) I let myself be swept away because . . . I loved you so.

TONY. (*Crosses to* ALICE.) Darling!

ALICE. No, wait, Tony. I want to make it clear to you. Listen, you're of a different world . . . a whole different kind of people. Oh I don't mean money or socially . . . that's too silly. But your family and mine . . . it just wouldn't work, Tony. It just wouldn't work. (ALICE *crosses to* R. *below* TONY.)

(*The sound of the outer door closing.*)

ED. (*Heard in hallway off stage.*) All right, have it your way. (*At the sound of the voice,* TONY *crosses to* L.) She can't dance. That's why they pay her all that money . . . because she can't dance. (ALICE *takes a few steps to* R.)

ESSIE. (*Still not in sight.*) Well, I don't call that dancing what she does. (*She appears in archway followed by* ED.) Oh, hello! How was the ballet? (*Throwing her hat on desk.*)

ALICE. It was fine, Essie.

TONY. Wonderful.

ED. (*Following into room after* ESSIE.) Hello there.

TONY. Hello.

ESSIE. Look, what do you people think? Ed and I just saw Fred Astaire and Ginger Rogers. Do you think she can dance, Mr. Kirby? (*Crossing over to* TONY.)

TONY. Why yes. I always thought so.

ESSIE. What does she *do* anyhow? (*Crossing to* TONY.) Now look, you're Fred Astaire, and I'm Ginger Rogers. (*Puts herself close to* TONY.)

ALICE. Essie, please!

ESSIE. I only want to use him for a minute. Now look, Mr. Kirby
. . . (*Putting her arms around* TONY'S *neck.*)

ALICE. Essie, you're just as good as Ginger Rogers. We all agree.

ESSIE. You see, Ed?

ED. (*Crossing to arch. Backing up.*) Yeh. . . . Come on, Essie . . .
we're butting in here.

ESSIE. Oh they've been together all evening. . . . (*Crosses up to
arch.*) Good night, Mr. Kirby. Good night, Alice.

TONY. Good night, Mrs. Carmichael.

ED. Good night. Essie, did you ask Grandpa about us having a baby?
(*Crossing up to stairs.*)

ESSIE. Oh yes—he said to go right ahead.

(*They are out of sight up stairs.*)

ALICE. (*Crossing L. to below table.*) You see, Tony? That's what it
would be like.

TONY. (*Crossing over to* ALICE.) Oh I didn't mind that. Anyhow,
we're not going to live with your family. It's just you and I.

ALICE. No it isn't . . . it's never quite that. I love them, Tony . . .
I love them deeply. Some people could break away, but I couldn't.
I know they do rather strange things. . . . But they're gay and
they're fun and . . . I don't know . . . there's a kind of nobility
about them.

TONY. Alice, you talk as though only you could understand them.
That's not true. Why every family has got curious little traits. What
of it? My father raises orchids at ten thousand dollars a bulb.
(ALICE *crosses up* R. *to back of chair.*) Is that sensible? My mother
believes in spiritualism. That's just as bad as your mother writing
plays, isn't it?

ALICE. It goes deeper, Tony. Your mother believes in spiritualism
because it's fashionable, and your father raises orchids because he
can afford to. My mother writes plays because eight years ago a typewriter was delivered here by mistake. (*She crosses to* R.)

TONY. Darling, what *of* it?

ALICE. (*Crossing back to chair.*) And—and look at Grandpa.
Thirty-five years ago he just quit business one day. He started up to
his office in the elevator and came right down again. He just
stopped. He could have been a rich man, (*Sitting* R. *of table.*) but
he said it took too much time. So for thirty-five years, he's just collected snakes, and gone to circuses and commencements. It never
occurs to any of them . . .

(GRANDPA *comes down stairs.*)

GRANDPA. (*Pausing in doorway.*) Hello there, children!

TONY. (*Turns to* GRANDPA.) Good evening, Mr. Vanderhof.

ALICE. Hello, Grandpa.

GRANDPA. (*Coming into the room.*) How's the weather? Looks like a nice summer evening.

ALICE. Yes, it's lovely, Grandpa.

GRANDPA. (*Starting up.*) Well, I'm off. Good-bye, Mr. Kirby . . . I've got a date with the policeman on the corner.

TONY. (*Crossing* U.S.) Policeman?

GRANDPA. We've got a standing date—twelve-thirty every night. Known him since he was a little boy. He's really a doctor, but after he graduated, he came to me and said he didn't want to be a doctor —he had always wanted to be a policeman. So I said, "You go ahead and be a policeman, if that's what you want to be," and that's what he did. . . . How do you like my new hat?

TONY. It's very nice, Mr. Vanderhof.

GRANDPA. (*Regarding hat.*) Yeh, I like it. The Government gave it to me. (*Exits* U.L.)

DONALD. (*Entering from kitchen* U.R. *with an accordion slung over his shoulder.*) Oh, excuse me. I didn't know you folks was in here.

ALICE. (*Resigned.*) It's all right, Donald.

DONALD. Rheba kind of fancied some candy and I . . . Oh, there it is. (*Crossing to buffet.*) You all don't want it, do you?

ALICE. No, Donald.

DONALD. (*Crossing to* R.) Thanks. . . . Did you have a nice evening?

ALICE. Yes, Donald.

DONALD. (*Edging over another step.*) Nice dinner?

ALICE. Yes, Donald.

DONALD. (*Another step to the* R.) Was the ballet nice?

ALICE. Yes, Donald.

DONALD. That's nice. (*He exits through kitchen door* R.)

ALICE. (*Rising.*) Now! Now, do you see what I mean? Could you explain Donald to your father? Could you explain Grandpa? You couldn't, Tony, you couldn't! I love you, Tony, but I love them too! And it's no use, Tony! It's no use! (*Crosses* R. *She is weeping now in spite of herself.*)

TONY. (*Takes her hands, quietly says.*) There's only one thing you've said that matters, that makes any sense at all. You love me.

ALICE. But, Tony, I know so well . . .

TONY. But, darling, don't you think other people have had the same problem? Everybody's got a family.

ALICE. (*Through her tears.*) But not like mine.

TONY. That doesn't stop people who love each other . . . Darling! Darling, won't you trust me and go on loving me, and forget everything else?

ALICE. How can I?

TONY. Because nothing can keep us apart. You know that. You must know it. They want you to be happy, don't they? They *must*.

ALICE. Of course they do. But they can't change, Tony. I wouldn't want them to change.

TONY. (*Releases her hands.*) They won't have to change. They're charming, lovable people, just as they are. Everything will work out . . . you're worrying about something that may never come up.

ALICE. Oh, Tony, am I?

TONY. All that matters right now is that we love each other. That's so, isn't it?

ALICE. (*Whispering.*) Yes.

TONY. Well, then! (*They embrace, sigh and kiss.*)

ALICE. (*In his arms.*) Tony, Tony!

TONY. (*As they break.*) Now! I'd like to see a little gayety around here. Young gentleman calling, and getting engaged and everything.

ALICE. (*Smiling up into his face.*) What do I say?

TONY. Well, first you thank the young man for getting engaged to you.

ALICE. (*Crossing to below table.*) Thank you, Mr. Kirby, for getting engaged to me.

TONY. (*Following her.*) And then you tell him what it was about him that first took your girlish heart.

ALICE. (*Leaning against table.*) The back of your head.

TONY. Huh?

ALICE. Uh-huh. It wasn't your charm, and it wasn't your money . . . it was the back of your head. I just liked it.

TONY. What happened when I turned around?

ALICE. Oh, I got used to it after a while.

TONY. (*Tenderly.*) Oh, Alice, think of it. We're pretty lucky, aren't we?

ALICE. I know that *I* am. I'm the luckiest girl in the world.

TONY. I'm not exactly unlucky myself. (*Holding her in his arms;*

kiss; sigh.) Oh, dear, I guess I ought to . . . (*Backing away. He looks at his watch.*) Good night, darling. Until tomorrow.

ALICE. (*Crosses to* TONY—*they kiss.*) Good night.

TONY. Isn't it wonderful we work in the same office? Otherwise I'd be hanging around *here* all day.

ALICE. (*Starts with* TONY *for the hall.*) Won't it be funny in the office tomorrow—seeing each other and just going on as though nothing had happened?

TONY. Thank God I'm vice-president. (*Turns up.*) I can dictate to you all day (*Accordion.*) "Dear Miss Sycamore: I love you, I love you, I love you." (*They embrace.*)

ALICE. Oh, darling! You're such a fool.

TONY. (*An arm about her as he starts toward hallway* U.L.) Why don't you meet me in the drugstore in the morning—before you go up to the office? I'll have millions of things to say to you. (*Picks up his hat as they head for the door.*)

ALICE. (*Off stage.*) All right.

TONY. And then lunch, and then dinner tomorrow night.

ALICE. Oh, Tony! What will people say?

TONY. It's got to come out sometime. In fact, if you know a good housetop, I'd like to do a little shouting. (*She laughs—a happy little ripple. They are out of sight in hallway by this time; their voices become inaudible.*)

(PAUL, *at this point, decides to call it a day down in the cellar. He comes through door, followed by* DE PINNA. *He is carrying a small metal container, filled with powder.*)

PAUL. (*Crossing to table* C.) Yes, sir, Mr. De Pinna, we did a good night's work.

DE PINNA. (*Following.*) That's what. Five hundred Black Panthers, three hundred Willow Trees, and eight dozen Junior Kiddie Bombers. (ALICE *comes back from hallway, still under the spell of her love.*)

PAUL. Pretty good! . . . Why, hello, Alice. You just come in?

ALICE. (*Softly; leans against wall.*) No. No, I've been home quite a while.

PAUL. Have a nice evening?

ALICE. (*Almost singing it.*) I had a beautiful evening, Father.

PAUL. Say, I'd like you to take a look at this new red fire. Will you turn out the lights, Mr. De Pinna? I want Alice to get the full effect.

(DE PINNA *goes up to switch.*)

ALICE. (*Who hasn't heard a word.*) What, Father?
PAUL. Take a look at this new red fire. It's beautiful. (DE PINNA *switches lights out;* PAUL *touches a match to the powder. The red fire blazes, shedding a soft glow over the room.*) There! What do you think of it? Isn't it beautiful?
ALICE. (*Radiant; her face aglow, her voice soft.*) Yes. Oh, Father, everything's beautiful, it's the most beautiful red fire in the world! (*She rushes to him and throws her arms about him, almost unable to bear her own happiness.*)

CURTAIN

ACT II

As curtain rises, GRANDPA *is seated* R. *of the table,* PAUL *above table, and a newcomer,* GAY WELLINGTON, *is seated* L. *of table.* PENNY *stands with one of her scripts at* L. *of table and* ED *is standing to* R. *of table.* DONALD *stands back of* GAY WELLINGTON *holding tray of used dinner dishes.* GAY *is drinking as curtain rises.* ED *stands* R. *holding type stick.*

GAY. All right, I said to him, you can take your old job . . . (*She drinks.*)

PENNY. I'm ready to read you the new play, Miss Wellington, any time you are.

GAY. (*Pours.*) Just a minute, dearie. Just a minute. (*Drinks again.*) (ED *preoccupied with type stick.*)

PENNY. The only thing is—I hope you won't mind my mentioning this, but—you don't drink when you're acting, do you, Miss Wellington? I'm just asking, of course.

GAY. (*Crossing to* PENNY.) I'm glad you brought it up. Once a play opens, I never touch a drop. Minute I enter a stage door, the bottle gets put away until intermission.

(RHEBA *enters* U.R. *and crosses down to table carrying a tray.*)

GRANDPA. Have you been on the stage a long time, Miss Wellington?

GAY. All my life. I've played everything. Ever see "Peg o' My Heart"?

GRANDPA. Yes.

GAY. I saw it too. Good show. . . . My! Hot night, ain't it?

DONALD. You want me to open the window, Miss Wellington?

GAY. No, the Hell with the weather. . . . Say, he's cute.

(RHEBA, *clearing table at this moment, throws* GAY *a black look, bangs a glass on her tray and exits* U.R.)

DONALD. (*Starting off after* RHEBA.) She's just acting, Rheba, that's all; she don't mean anything. (*Exits* U.R.)

PENNY. (*Making the best of it, crossing over to her desk.*) Well, any time you're ready, we'll go up to my room and start. I thought

36

I'd read the play up in my room. (*Crosses up to stairs.*) (ED *drifts up to xylophone.*)

GAY. (*Circling U.S.—takes glass from table.*) All right, dearie, I'm ready. (*Suddenly her gaze becomes transfixed. She shakes her head as though to dislodge the image, then looks again and receives verification. Puts gin bottle and glass on table.*) When I see snakes, it's time to lay down. (*She makes for couch R.*) (ESSIE *starts downstairs.*)

PENNY. (*Crossing back of table to couch.*) Oh dear! Oh dear! Oh, but those are real, Miss Wellington! (DONALD *enters up R. bearing a tray.* PAUL *rises.*) They're Grandpa's. Those are real! (GAY *has passed right out cold.*) Oh, dear! I hope she is not going to —— Miss Wellington!

ED. (*Crossing up to hand press.*) She's out like a light.

PAUL. (*Crossing U.S. a step.*) Better let her sleep it off.

DONALD. Rheba, Miss Wellington just passed out. (*Exits U.R.*)

RHEBA. (*Off stage.*) Good.

PENNY. Do you think she'll be all right?

GRANDPA. Yes, but I wouldn't cast her in the religious play.

PENNY. Well, I suppose I'll just have to wait.

(ED *bangs the hand press.* ESSIE *crosses down to chair L. of table.*)

GRANDPA. Next time you meet an actress on the top of a bus, Penny, I think I'd *send* her the play instead of bringing her home to read it.

(*Another bang.* PENNY *covers* GAY *with couch cover.*)

ESSIE. Ed, I wish you'd stop printing and take those "Love Dreams" around. You've got to get back in time to play for me when Kolenkhov comes. (*A bang of the hand press again.*)

GRANDPA. Kolenkhov coming tonight? (*Goes to bookcase for stamp album and returns to table.*)

ESSIE. (*Executing a few toe steps.*) Yes, tomorrow night's his night, but I had to change it on account of Alice.

GRANDPA. Oh! . . . Big doings around here tomorrow night, huh?

PENNY. (*Crossing to desk.*) Isn't it exciting? You know I'm so nervous—you'd think it was me he was engaged to instead of Alice. (*Sitting in desk chair. Takes script and pencil.*) (GRANDPA *busies himself with album.*)

ESSIE. (*Doing leg exercise. She is L. of table.*) What do you think they'll *be* like—his mother and father? . . . Ed, what are you doing now?

37

ED. (*Coming down.*) Penny, did you see the new mask I made last night? (*He reveals a new side of his character by suddenly holding a homemade mask before his face.*) Guess who it is?

PENNY. Don't tell me now, Ed. Wait a minute. . . . Helen of Troy?

ED. (*Disappointed.*) It's Mrs. Roosevelt. (ESSIE *on toes.* ED *puts mask down and exits into kitchen.*) (PAUL, *meanwhile, comes* D.R. *from buffet with a steel-like contraption in his hand. It's a Meccano set model of the Queen Mary. He puts it down on floor and proceeds to sit down beside it.*)

PAUL. You know the nice thing about these Meccano sets, you can make so many different things with them. Last week it was the Empire State Building.

GRANDPA. What is it this week?

PAUL. Queen Mary.

GRANDPA. Hasn't got the right hat on.

(DE PINNA *enters from* R. *of hall.* PENNY *sits.* ED *comes in from kitchen bringing a pile of candy boxes beautifully wrapped and tied together for purposes of delivery. He crosses to* U.C.)

ED. . . . Look, Mr. De Pinna—would you open the door and see if there's a man standing in front of the house?

DE PINNA. Why, what for?

ED. Well, the last two days, when I've been out delivering candy, I think a man's been following me.

ESSIE. Ed, you're crazy.

ED. No, I'm not. He follows me, and he stands and watches the house.

DE PINNA. Really? (*Striding out.*) I'll take a look and see.

GRANDPA. I don't see what anybody would follow *you* for, Ed.

PENNY. Well, there's a lot of kidnapping going on, Grandpa.

GRANDPA. Yes, but not of Ed.

ED. (*As* DE PINNA *returns from hall* U.L.) Well? Did you see him?

DE PINNA. There's nobody out there at all.

ED. You're sure?

DE PINNA. Positive. I just saw him walk away.

(PAUL *puts the model back on the buffet.*)

ED. You see?

ESSIE. Oh, it might have been anybody, walking along the street. Ed, will you hurry and get back? (PAUL *starts* D.R.)

ED. (*Picking up his boxes* U.C.) Oh, all right. (*Exits* U.L.)

DE PINNA. (*Crossing to* R. *below table.*) Want to go down now, Mr. Sycamore, and finish packing up the fireworks?

PAUL. Yeh, we've got to take the stuff up to Mt. Vernon in the morning. (PAUL *and* DE PINNA *exit* D.R.)

(*The voice of* ALICE, *happily singing, is heard as she descends stairs.*)

ALICE. (*As she comes into the room, finishing song.*) Mother, may I borrow some paper? I'm making out a list for Rheba tomorrow night.

PENNY. Yes, dear. (*Drunken mutter from* GAY.) Here's some.

ALICE. (*Crossing to table. As she sights* GAY.) Why, what happened to your actress friend? Is she giving a performance?

PENNY. No, she's not acting, Alice. She's really drunk. (ESSIE *dances to* R. *of* GRANDPA'S *chair.*)

ALICE. Essie, dear, you're going to give Rheba the kitchen all day tomorrow, aren't you? Because she'll need it.

ESSIE. Of course, Alice. I'm going to start some Love Dreams now, so I'll be 'way ahead. (*She goes into kitchen* U.R.)

ALICE. Thanks, dear. . . . (*Crossing to* PENNY.) Look, Mother, I'm coming home at three o'clock tomorrow. Will you have everything down in the cellar by that time? The typewriter, and the snakes, and the xylophone, and the printing press . . .

GRANDPA. And Miss Wellington.

ALICE. And Miss Wellington. That'll give me time to arrange the table, and fix the flowers.

GRANDPA. The Kirbys are certainly going to get the wrong impression of this house.

ALICE. You'll do all that, won't you, Mother?

PENNY. Of course, dear. . . . (*Turns.*)

ALICE. . . . And I think we'd better have cocktails ready by seven-fifteen, in case they happen to come a little early. . . . I wonder if I ought to let Rheba cook the dinner. What do you think, Grandpa?

GRANDPA. Now, Alice, I wouldn't worry. From what I've seen of the boy I'm sure the Kirbys are very nice people, and if everything isn't so elaborate tomorrow night, it's all right too.

ALICE. (*Crossing to back of table.*) Darling, I'm not trying to impress them, or pretend we're anything that we aren't. I just want everything to—to go off well.

GRANDPA. (*Putting his hand over* ALICE'S.) No reason why it shouldn't, Alice.

PENNY. We're all going to do everything we can to make it a nice party.

ALICE. (*Crossing to* L.) Oh, my darlings, I love you. You're the most wonderful family in the world, and I'm the happiest girl in the world. I didn't know anyone could be so happy. Why, this past week has been like—floating. He's so wonderful, Grandpa. (*Crossing to back of table.*) Why, just seeing him—you don't know what it does to me.

GRANDPA. Just seeing him. Just seeing him for lunch, and dinner, and until four o'clock in the morning, and at nine o'clock *next* morning you're at the office again and there he is. Just seeing him, huh?

ALICE. I don't care! I'm in love! (*Kisses* GRANDPA *and starts for* U.R. *She swings open kitchen door.*) Rheba! Rheba! (*She goes into kitchen.*)

GRANDPA. Nice, isn't it? Nice to see her so happy.

PENNY. (*Rises—crosses to table.*) Yes, I remember when I was engaged to Paul—how happy I was. And you know, I still feel that way.

GRANDPA. I know. . . . Nice the way Ed and Essie get along too, isn't it?

PENNY. And Donald and Rheba, even though they're *not* married. . . . Do you suppose Mr. De Pinna will ever marry anyone, Grandpa?

GRANDPA. (*A gesture toward couch.*) Well, there's Miss Wellington.

PENNY. Oh, dear, I *wish* she'd wake up. If we're going to read the play tonight ——

(DE PINNA *comes up from cellar,* D.R., *bringing along a rather large-sized unframed painting.*)

DE PINNA. Mrs. Sycamore, look what I found! (*He turns canvas around, revealing a portrait of a somewhat lumpy and largely naked discus thrower.*) Remember? (*He props picture on chair above table.*)

PENNY. (*Backs away.*) Why, of course. It's my painting of you as The Discus Thrower. Look, Grandpa.

GRANDPA. I remember it. Say, you've gotten a little bald, haven't you, Mr. De Pinna?

DE PINNA. (*Running a hand over his completely hairless head.*) Is it very noticeable? Well, there's still some right here.

PENNY. Well, it was a long time ago—just before I stopped painting. Let me see—that's eight years.

DE PINNA. Too bad you never finished it, Mrs. Sycamore. (*Crosses* D.R.)

PENNY. (*Looking back at picture.*) I always meant to finish it, Mr. De Pinna, but I just started to write a play one day and that was that. I never painted again.

GRANDPA. Just as well, too. *I* was going to have to strip next.

DE PINNA. (*Meditatively.*) My goodness, who would have thought, that day I came to deliver the ice, that I was going to stay here for eight years?

GRANDPA. The milkman was here for five, just ahead of you.

DE PINNA. Say, why did he leave, anyhow? I forget.

GRANDPA. He didn't leave. He died.

DE PINNA. Oh, yes. (*Crossing* R.)

PENNY. He was such a nice man. Remember the funeral, Grandpa? We never knew his name and it was kind of hard to get a certificate.

GRANDPA. What was the name we finally made up for him?

PENNY. Martin Vanderhof. We gave him *your* name.

GRANDPA. Oh, yes, I remember. (*Rises and goes up to alcove.*) (DE PINNA *lights pipe.*)

PENNY. It was a lovely thought, because otherwise he never would have got all those flowers.

GRANDPA. (*Coming down.*) Certainly was. And it didn't hurt *me* any. Not bothered with mail any more, and I haven't had a telephone call from that day to this. (*Business of catching fly on painting and feeding it to snakes. Returns to his chair; sits, reads paper.*)

PENNY. Yes, it was really a wonderful idea.

DE PINNA. (*Points to picture.*) I wish you'd finish that sometime, Mrs. Sycamore. I'd kind of like to have it.

PENNY. You know what, Mr. De Pinna? I think I'll do some work on it. Right tonight.

DE PINNA. Say! Will you? (*Door bell.*)

PENNY. (*Peering at the prostrate* GAY.) I don't think she's going to wake up anyhow. . . . Look, Mr. De Pinna! You go down in the cellar—(RHEBA *enters* U.R., *crosses to hall door.*)—and put on your costume. And bring up the easel. (DE PINNA *starts* R.) Is it still down there?

DE PINNA. (*Excited.*) I think so! (*He exits* D.R.)

PENNY. (*Crossing to stairs.*) Now, where did I put my palette and brushes?

(*The voice of* KOLENKHOV *is heard at door, booming as usual.*)

KOL. Rhebishka! My little Rhebishka!

RHEBA. (*Delighted, as usual.*) Yassuh, Mr. Kolenkhov!

PENNY. (*As she goes up stairs.*) Hello, Mr. Kolenkhov. Essie's in the kitchen.

KOL. Madame Sycamore, I greet you! (*His great arm again encircling* RHEBA, *he drags her protestingly into room.*) Tell me, Grandpa—what should I do about Rhebishka! I keep telling her she would make a great toe dancer—(*Breaking away, she laughs.*)—but she laughs only!

RHEBA. (*Starts off for* U.R.) No, suh! I couldn't get up on my toes, Mr. Kolenkhov! I got corns! (*She goes into kitchen.*)

KOL. (*Calling after her.*) Rhebishka, you could wear diamonds! (*Throws his hat on buffet.*) A great girl, Grandpa. (*Suddenly he sights portrait of* DE PINNA.) What is that?

GRANDPA. It's a picture of Mr. De Pinna. Penny painted it.

KOL. (*Summing it up.*) It stinks. (*Sits* L. *of table.*)

GRANDPA. I know. (*He indicates figure on couch.*) How do you like that?

KOL. (*Half rising. Peering over.*) What is *that*?

GRANDPA. She's an actress. Friend of Penny's. (GAY *mutters.*)

KOL. She is drunk—no?

GRANDPA. She is drunk—yes. . . . How are *you,* Kolenkhov?

KOL. Magnificent! Life is chasing around inside of me, like a squirrel.

GRANDPA. 'Tis, huh? . . . What's new in Russia? Any more letters from your friend in Moscow?

KOL. (*Nods.*) I have just heard from him. I saved for you the stamp.

GRANDPA. Thanks, Kolenkhov.

KOL. They have sent him to Siberia.

GRANDPA. They have, eh? How's he like it?

KOL. He has escaped. He has escaped and gone back to Moscow. He will get them yet if they do not get him. The Soviet Government! I could take the whole Soviet Government and—grrah! (*He crushes Stalin and all in one great paw, just as* ESSIE *comes in from kitchen* U.R. KOLENKHOV *rises.*)

ESSIE. I'm sorry I'm late, Mr. Kolenkhov. I'll get into my dancing clothes right away.

KOL. (*Crossing up to stairs.*) Tonight you will really work, Pav-

Iowa. (*As* ESSIE *goes up stairs.*) Tonight we will take something new.

GRANDPA. Essie making any progress, Kolenkhov?

KOL. (*First making elaborately sure that* ESSIE *is gone, then in a voice that would carry to Long Island.*) Confidentially, she stinks! (*Lights cigarette.*)

GRANDPA. Well, as long as she's having fun . . .

(DONALD *ambles in from kitchen, chuckling, carrying tray. He crosses down to table.*)

DONALD. You sure do tickle Rheba, Mr. Kolenkhov. She's laughing her head off out there. (*Gathers up remaining cups, bottle and glass.*)

KOL. (*Sits* L. *of table.*) She is a great woman. . . . Donald, what do you think of the Soviet Government?

DONALD. (*Puzzled.*) The what, Mr. Kolenkhov?

KOL. (*Gesture.*) I withdraw the question. What do you think of *this* Government?

DONALD. Oh, I like it fine. I'm on relief, you know.

KOL. Oh, yes. And you like it?

DONALD. Yassuh, it's fine. (*Starts to go* R.) Only thing is you got to go round to the place every week to get it, and sometimes you got to stand in line pretty near half an hour. Government ought to be run better than that—don't you think, Grandpa?

GRANDPA. (*As he fishes envelope out of his pocket. Opens letter.*) Government ought to stop sending me letters. Want me to be at the United States Marshal's office Tuesday morning at ten o'clock. Look at that. (*Throws letter to* KOLENKHOV.)

KOL. (*Peering at letter.*) Ah! Income tax! They have got you, Grandpa.

GRANDPA. (*Puts letter back in pocket.*) Mm. I'm supposed to give 'em a lot of money so as to keep Donald on relief.

DONALD. You don't say, Grandpa? *You going* to pay it from now on?

GRANDPA. That's what they want.

DONALD. You mean I can come right *here* and get it instead of standing in that line?

GRANDPA. No, Donald. I'm afraid you will have to waste a full half hour of your time every week.

DONALD. Well, I don't like it. It breaks up my week. (*Exits* U.R.)

KOL. He should have been in Russia when the Revolution came.

Then he would have stood in line . . . a bread line. Ah, Grandpa, what they have done to Russia. Think of it! The Grand Duchess Olga Katrina, a cousin of the Czar, she is a waitress in Childs' Restaurant! I ordered baked beans from her, only yesterday. It broke my heart. A crazy world, Grandpa.

GRANDPA. Oh, the world's not so crazy, Kolenkhov. It's the people *in* it. Life's pretty simple if you just relax.

KOL. (*Rising, crosses* U.C.) How can you relax in times like these?

GRANDPA. Well, if they'd relax there wouldn't *be* times like these. That's just my point. Life is kind of beautiful if you let it come to you. (*Crossing to buffet for his target and darts.*) But the trouble is, people forget that. I know I did. I was right in the thick of it . . . fighting, and scratching and clawing. Regular jungle. One day it just kind of struck me, I wasn't having any fun. (GRANDPA, *having hung his target on cellar door, returns to table.*)

KOL. So you did what?

GRANDPA. (*Standing below the table.*) Just relaxed. Thirty-five years ago, that was. And I've been a happy man ever since. (*Throws a dart and sits.*)

ALICE. (*Entering from kitchen.*) Good evening, Mr. Kolenkhov.

KOL. (*Crossing up to* ALICE C., *he bows low over her hand.*) Ah, Miss Alice! I have not seen you to present my congratulations.

ALICE. Thank you.

KOL. May you be very happy and have many children. That is my prayer for you.

ALICE. That's quite a thought. (*She exits up stairs, humming a fragment of song.*)

KOL. (*Crossing down.*) Ah, love! Love is all that is left in the world, Grandpa.

GRANDPA. Yes, but there is plenty of that.

KOL. And soon Stalin will take that away, too, I tell you, Grandpa . . .

(PENNY *enters down stairs. She has on an artist's smock over her dress, a flowing black tie, and a large blue velvet tam-o'-shanter, worn at a rakish angle. She carries a palette and an assortment of paints and brushes.*)

PENNY. Seems so nice to get into my art things again. They still look all right, don't they, Grandpa?

GRANDPA. Yes, indeed.

KOL. You are a breath of Paris, Madame Sycamore.

44

(DONALD *enters* U.R., *table cover over his arm.*)

PENNY. Oh, thank you, Mr. Kolenkhov.

DONALD. I didn't know you was working for the WPA.

PENNY. Oh, no, Donald. You see, I used to paint all the time —— (*The outer door slams and* ED *comes in.*)

ED. (*In considerable excitement.*) It happened again! There was a fellow following me every place I went!

PENNY. Nonsense, Ed. It's your imagination.

ED. No, it isn't. It happens every time I go out to deliver candy.

GRANDPA. Maybe he wants a piece of candy.

ED. It's all right for you *to laugh,* Grandpa, but he keeps following me.

KOL. (*Somberly.*) You do not know what following is. In Russia *everybody* is followed. I was followed right out of Russia.

PENNY. Of course. You see, Ed—the whole thing is just imagination.

(DE PINNA *comes up from cellar, ready for posing. He is carrying Roman toga, headband and sandals. Taking off coat as he goes up to alcove.*)

ED. (*Crosses to* L. *of alcove.*) Well, maybe. (*Takes off coat.*)

(DONALD *removes napkins and tablecloth and spreads table cover. Puts cover on* U.S. *chair.*)

PENNY. (PENNY'S *easel, a discus, and a small platform for posing purposes and Racing Form.*) Ah, here we are!

DE PINNA. (*Crosses to* D.L., *places easel.*) Where do you want this? Over there?

PENNY. (*Putting portrait on the easel.*) Put it here, Mr. De Pinna. (DE PINNA *strikes a pose on the model stand.*)

KOL. Ed, for tonight's lesson we use the first movement of Scheherazade.

ED. Okay.

PENNY. (*Studying* DE PINNA'S *figure.*) Mr. De Pinna, has something happened to your figure during these eight years?

DE PINNA. (*Pulling in his stomach.*) No, I don't think it's any different. (*With a sudden snort,* GAY *comes to.* DE PINNA *breaks pose and looks at* GAY.)

PENNY. (*Crossing to below table. Immediately alert.*) Yes, Miss Wellington? Yes? (*For answer,* GAY *peers first at* PENNY, *then at* DE PINNA.)

GAY. Wo-o-o! (*And with that she goes right back to sleep.*)
PENNY. (*Exchanges look with* DE PINNA *and then returns to her painting.*) Oh, dear.

(ESSIE *comes tripping down stairs—very much the ballet dancer. She is in full costume—ballet skirt, tight white satin bodice, a garland of roses in her hair.*)

ESSIE. (*Crossing to xylophone.*) Sorry, Mr. Kolenkhov. I couldn't find my slippers.
KOL. (*Coming down. Having previously removed his coat, he now takes off his shirt, displaying an enormous hairy chest beneath his undershirt.*) We have a hot night for it, my Pavlowa, but art is only achieved through perspiration. (*Back to alcove.*)
PENNY. Why, that's wonderful, Mr. Kolenkhov. Did you hear that, Grandpa—art is only achieved through perspiration.
GRANDPA. (ESSIE *fixes slippers during this.*) Yes, but it helps if you've got a little talent with it. (*He takes up a handful of feathered darts.*) Only made two bull's-eyes last night. Got to do better than that. (*He hurls a dart at board, then his eye travels to* GAY, *whose posterior offers an even easier target. Looks to* PENNY *for approval. Then returns to his game and hurls one more dart and sits. Reads his paper.*) (ED *strikes a few notes.*)
KOL. You are ready? We begin! (*With a gesture he orders the music started; under* KOLENKHOV'S *critical eye* ESSIE *begins the mazes of the dance. Meanwhile* DE PINNA'S *free hand now holds a copy of Racing Form, the total effect being a trifle un-Grecian.*) Now! Pirouette! Pirouette! (ESSIE *hesitates.*) Come, come! You can do that! It's eight years now! (ESSIE *pirouettes.*) At last! Entre chat! Entre chat! (DONALD *crosses* U.R. ESSIE *leaps into the air, her feet twirling.* KOLENKHOV *turns to* GRANDPA.) No, Grandpa, you cannot relax with Stalin in Russia. The Czar relaxed, and what happened to *him?*
GRANDPA. He was too late!
ESSIE. (*Still leaping away.*) Mr. Kolenkhov! Mr. Kolenkhov!
KOL. If he had not relaxed the Grand Duchess Olga Katrina would not be selling baked beans today.
ESSIE. (*Imploringly.*) Mr. Kolenkhov!
KOL. I'm sorry. We go back to the pirouette.
PENNY. Could you pull in your stomach, Mr. De Pinna? (*Door bell.*) That's right.

KOL. A little freer. A little freer with the hands. The whole body must work. Ed, help us with the music. (RHEBA *enters* U.R. *Crosses to hall door*.) The music must be free, too. (*By way of guiding* ED, KOLENKHOV *hums the music at the pace that it should go. He is even pirouetting a bit himself*.) (*From the front door comes the murmur of voices, not quite audible over the music. Then the stunned figure of* RHEBA *comes into archway, her eyes popping*.)

RHEBA. (*Heavy whisper*.) Mrs. Sycamore . . . Mrs. Sycamore.

PENNY. What, Rheba?

(RHEBA *edges over* R. *With a gesture that has a grim foreboding in it, motions toward the still invisible reason for her panic. There is a second's pause, and then the reason is revealed in all its horror. The* KIRBYS, *in full evening dress, stand in archway. All three of them,* MR. *and* MRS. KIRBY, *and* TONY. DE PINNA *rushes to cellar door carrying his model stand with him.* KOLENKHOV *runs to alcove to squirm into his shirt and coat.* ESSIE *makes for alcove, also.* ED *pushes xylophone in place and hastily dons his coat.* RHEBA *crosses to buffet.* DONALD *comes* D.R. *still carrying soiled dinner linen.* PENNY *utters a stifled gasp; she puts the painting against wall with the easel. Then removes her smock and tam.* GRANDPA, *alone of them all, rises to the situation. With a kind of old world grace, he puts down his newspaper and makes the guests welcome*.)

TONY. Good evening.

GRANDPA. (*Rising and crossing to back of table*.) How do you do?

KIRBY. (*Uncertainly*.) How do you do?

TONY. Are we too early?

GRANDPA. No, no. Come right in. It's perfectly all right—we're glad to see you. (*His eyes still on the* KIRBYS, *he gives* DONALD *a good push toward kitchen, by way of a hint*.) (DONALD *goes, promptly, with a quick little stunned whistle that sums up his feelings.* RHEBA *looking back exits* U.R.)

PENNY. Why—yes. Only—we thought it was to be tomorrow night.

MRS. KIRBY. Tomorrow night!

KIRBY. What!

GRANDPA. Now, it's perfectly all right. Just make yourselves at home. (*Crossing to back of table. Placing chair*.)

KIRBY. Tony, how could you possibly ——

TONY. I—I don't know. I thought ——

MRS. KIRBY. Really, Tony! This is most embarrassing.

GRANDPA. Not at all. Why, we weren't doing a thing.

47

PENNY. No, no. Just a quiet evening at home.

GRANDPA. That's all. . . . Now don't let it bother you. This is Alice's mother, Mrs. Sycamore.

PENNY. How do you do.

GRANDPA. . . . Alice's sister, Mrs. Carmichael . . . *Mr.* Carmichael . . . Mr. Kolenkhov. (KOLENKHOV *comes down, bows and discovers his shirt tail exposed. Thrusts it into his trousers. At this point* DE PINNA *takes an anticipatory step forward, and* GRANDPA *is practically compelled to perform the introduction. Crossing to* DE PINNA.) And—Mr. De Pinna.

THE KIRBYS. How do you do?

DE PINNA. Don't mind my costume. I'll take it right off.

GRANDPA. Mr. De Pinna, would you tell Mr. Sycamore to come right up? Tell him that Mr. and Mrs. Kirby are here.

PENNY. (*Her voice a heavy whisper.*) And be sure to put his pants on.

DE PINNA. (*Whispering right back.*) All right. . . . Excuse me. (*He vanishes—discus, Racing Form, and all—*D.R.) (*At this point* PENNY *hastily throws a couch cover over* GAY. PENNY *pushes* GAY'S *posterior with her knee.* GRANDPA, *crossing* R., *places chair.*)

MRS. KIRBY. (*Crossing to* GRANDPA'S *chair.*) Thank you.

PENNY. (*Crossing to arch* U.L.) I'll tell Alice that you're —— (*She is at foot of stairs.*) Alice! Alice, dear! (KIRBY *comes* D.L. *The voice of* ALICE *from above, "What is it?"*) Alice, will you come down, dear? We've got a surprise for you. (*She comes back into the room, summoning all her charm.*) Well!

GRANDPA. Mrs. Kirby, may I take your wrap? (*Removes it.*)

MRS. KIRBY. Well—thank you. If you're perfectly sure (*She turns.*) that we're not —— (*Suddenly she sees snakes and lets out a scream.*)

GRANDPA. Oh, don't be alarmed, Mrs. Kirby. They're perfectly harmless.

MRS. KIRBY. Thank you. (*She sinks into a chair, weakly.*)

GRANDPA. Ed, take 'em into the kitchen.

(TONY *takes his father's hat to hall and returns to the room.* ED *at once obeys. Takes snake solarium to kitchen.*)

PENNY. (*Putting Japanese bowl* C. *of buffet.*) Of course we're so used to them around the house ——

MRS. KIRBY. I'm sorry to trouble you, but snakes happen to be ——

48

KIRBY. I feel very uncomfortable about this. Tony, how could you have done such a thing?

TONY. I'm sorry, Dad. I thought it was tonight.

KIRBY. It was very careless of you. *Very!*

PENNY. Oh, now, anybody can get mixed up, Mr. Kirby.

GRANDPA. Penny, how about some dinner for these folks? They've come for dinner, you know.

MRS. KIRBY. Oh, please don't bother. (ED *enters* U.R.) We're really not hungry at all.

PENNY. (*Crosses to* ED.) But it's not a bit of bother. Ed!— (*Her voice drops to a loud whisper.*) Ed, tell Donald to run down to the A. and P. and get half a dozen bottles of beer, and—ah—some canned salmon —— (*Her voice comes up again.*) Do you like canned salmon, Mr. Kirby?

KIRBY. (*A step in to* R.) Please don't trouble, Mrs. Sycamore. I have a little indigestion, anyway.

PENNY. Oh, I'm sorry. . . . How about you, Mrs. Kirby? Do you like canned salmon?

MRS. KIRBY. (*You just know that she hates it.*) Oh, I'm very fond of it.

PENNY. You can have frankfurters if you'd rather.

MRS. KIRBY. (*Regally.*) Either one will do.

PENNY. (*To* ED *again.*) Well, make it frankfurters and some canned corn, and Campbell's Soup —— (ED *crosses* U.R. *to door,* PENNY *following.*) Got that, Ed?

ED. (*Going out kitchen door* U.R.) Okay!

PENNY. (*Calling after him.*) And tell him to hurry! (PENNY *again addresses the* KIRBYS. *Comes down* R.) The A. and P. is just at the corner, and frankfurters don't take *any* time to boil.

GRANDPA. (*As* PAUL *comes through cellar door* D.R.) And this is Alice's father, *Mr.* Sycamore. Mr. and Mrs. Kirby.

THE KIRBYS. How do you do?

PAUL. I hope you'll forgive my appearance.

(ALICE *starts down stairs.*)

PENNY. This is Mr. Sycamore's busiest time of the year. Just before the Fourth of July he always ——

(*And then* ALICE *comes down. She is a step into the room before she realizes what has happened; then she fairly freezes in her tracks.*)

49

ALICE. (*At arch.*) Oh!

TONY. (*Crossing up to her.*) Darling, I'm the most dull-witted person in the world. I thought it was tonight.

ALICE. (*Staggered.*) Why, Tony, I thought you —— (*To the* KIRBYS. *Coming* D.L. *of table.*) I'm so sorry—I can't imagine—why, I wasn't—have you all met each other?

KIRBY. Yes, indeed.

MRS. KIRBY. How do you do, Alice?

ALICE. (*Not even yet in control of herself.*) How do you do, Mrs. Kirby? I'm afraid I'm not very—presentable.

TONY. (*Crossing down to* ALICE.) Darling, you look lovely.

KIRBY. (*A step toward* ALICE.) Of course she does. Don't let this upset you, my dear—we've all just met each other a night sooner, that's all.

MRS. KIRBY. Of course.

ALICE. But I was planning such a nice party tomorrow night. . . .

KIRBY. (*Being the good fellow.*) Well, we'll come again tomorrow night.

TONY. There you are, Alice. Am I forgiven?

ALICE. I guess so. It's just that I —— We'd better see about getting you some dinner.

PENNY. Oh, that's all done, Alice. (DONALD, *hat in hand, comes through kitchen door; hurries across room and out front way. He is followed into room by* ED, *who joins the family circle.* GRANDPA *crosses to back of table.*) That's all been attended to.

(*Door slams on* DONALD'S *exit.*)

ALICE. (*Sensing that* DONALD *is on way to round up a meal crosses over to* PENNY.) But Mother—what did you send out for? Because Mr. Kirby suffers from indigestion—he can only eat certain things.

KIRBY. (*Crossing to* L. *of table.*) Oh, it's all right. It's all right.

TONY. Of course it is, darling.

PENNY. I asked him what he wanted, Alice.

ALICE. (*Doubtfully.*) Yes, but ——

KIRBY. Now, now, it's not as serious as all that. Just because I have a little indigestion.

KOL. (*Coming down to* R. *of table.*) Perhaps it is not indigestion at all, Mr. Kirby. Perhaps you have stomach ulcers.

ALICE. Don't be absurd, Mr. Kolenkhov!

GRANDPA. You mustn't mind Mr. Kolenkhov, Mr. Kirby. He's a Russian, and Russians are inclined to look on the dark side.

KOL. All right, I am a Russian. But a friend of mine, a Russian, *died* from stomach ulcers.

KIRBY. Really, I ——

ALICE. (*Desperately.*) Please, Mr. Kolenkhov! Mr. Kirby has indigestion and that's all. (PAUL *drifts up to* R. *of buffet.*)

KOL. (*With a Russian shrug.*) All right, let him wait. (*Crossing over to* R.)

GRANDPA. Do sit down, Mr. Kirby. Make yourself comfortable.

KIRBY. Thank you. (*He sits* L. *of table.*)

PENNY. (*Sitting above table.*) Well —— (*She sighs; a pause, a general shifting.*) (PAUL *drifts* U.R. ALICE *joins* TONY L.)

GRANDPA. (*Coming* D.S. *Leaping into the breach.*) Tell me, Mr. Kirby, how do you find business conditions? Are we pretty well out of the depression?

KIRBY. What? . . . Yes, I think so. Of course, it all depends.

GRANDPA. But you figure that things are going to keep on improving?

KIRBY. Broadly speaking, yes. As a matter of fact, industry is now operating at sixty-four per cent of full capacity, as against eighty-two per cent in 1925. (GAY *rises.*) Of course, in 1929 ——

GAY. (*She weaves unsteadily across room singing—"There was a young lady from Wheeling who had a remarkable feeling."* ALICE *crosses* D.L. *The imposing figure of* KIRBY *intrigues* GAY.) Wo-o-o —— (*She pinches his cheeks and with that lunges on her way up stairs.*)

PENNY. She—ah ——

(*The* KIRBYS, *of course, are considerably astounded by this exhibition. The* SYCAMORES *have watched it with varying degrees of frozen horror.* ALICE *in particular is speechless; it is* GRANDPA *who comes to her rescue.*)

GRANDPA. (*Crossing to back of table.*) That may seem a little strange to you people, but she's not quite accountable for her actions. A friend of Mrs. Sycamore's. She came to dinner and was overcome by the heat. (*Sits above table.*)

PENNY. Yes, some people feel it, you know, more than others. Perhaps I'd better see if she's all right. Excuse me please? (*She goes hastily up stairs.*)

ALICE. (*Crossing to* L. *of table.*) It *is* awfully hot. (*A fractional pause.*) You usually escape all this hot weather, don't you, Mrs. Kirby? Up in Maine?

MRS. KIRBY. (*On the frigid side.*) As a rule. I had to come down this week, however, for the Flower Show.

TONY. Mother wouldn't miss that for the world. That blue ribbon is the high spot of her year.

ESSIE. (*Crossing down to R. of table.*) I won a ribbon at a Flower Show once. For raising onions. Remember, Alice?

ALICE. (*Quickly.*) That was a Garden Show, Essie.

ESSIE. (*Crosses to couch.*) Oh, yes. (PENNY *comes bustling down stairs again* U.L. *Comes* D.L. KIRBY *rises.*)

PENNY. I think she'll be all right now. . . . Has Donald come back yet?

ALICE. No, he hasn't.

PENNY. Well, he'll be right back, and it won't take any time at all. I'm afraid you must be starved.

KIRBY. (*Going* U.C.) Oh, no. Quite all right. (*He sees* PAUL'S *Meccano boat model.*) Hello! What's this? I didn't know there were little children in the house.

PAUL. Oh, no. That's mine.

KIRBY. Really? Well, I suppose every man has his hobby. Or do you use this as a model of some kind?

PAUL. No, I just play with it.

KIRBY. I see.

TONY. Maybe you'd be better off if *you* had a hobby like that, Dad. Instead of raising orchids.

KIRBY. (*Crossing down to back of table. Indulgently.*) Yes, I wouldn't be surprised. (PENNY *sits* L. *of table.* ALICE *comes down* R.)

ALICE. (*Leaping on this as a safe topic.*) Oh, *do* tell us about your orchids, Mr. Kirby. (KIRBY *crosses up to alcove.* ALICE *addresses others.*) You know, they take six years before they blossom, don't they? Think of that!

KIRBY. (*Addressing* GRANDPA *and* PENNY. *Warming to his subject.*) Oh, some of them take longer than that. I've got one coming along now that I've waited *ten* years for.

PENNY. (*Making a joke.*) Believe it or not, I was waiting for an orchid. (PAUL *laughs.*)

KIRBY. (ESSIE *sits.*) Ah—yes. Of course during that time they require the most scrupulous care. (*The sound of hall door closing and* DONALD *suddenly bulges through* U.L. *archway, his arms full. The tops of beer bottles and two or three large cucumbers peep over the tops of the huge paper bag.*) I remember a bulb that I was very fond of ——

ALICE. (*Crossing up to* DONALD.) Donald!

PENNY. (*Rising and going to* DONALD.) Ah, here we are! Did you get everything, Donald?

DONALD. Yes'm. Only they didn't have any frankfurters, so I got pickled pig's feet. (*Exits* U.R.)

(KIRBY *blanches at the very idea. He crosses to* L. *below the table.* ED *sits* U.S. *end of couch.*)

ALICE. (*Following* DONALD *to kitchen door. Taking command.*) Never mind, Donald—just bring everything into the kitchen. (*She turns at kitchen door.*) Mr. Kirby, please tell them *all* about the orchids—I know they'd love to hear it. And—excuse me. (*She goes* U.R.) (PENNY *crosses, looks off into kitchen, and comes down* R. *of table.*)

GRANDPA. Kind of an expensive hobby, isn't it, Mr. Kirby—raising orchids?

KIRBY. (*Sits* L. *of table.*) Yes, it is, but I feel that if a hobby gives one sufficient pleasure, it's never expensive.

GRANDPA. That's very true. (PAUL, ESSIE *and* ED *are sitting on the couch.* TONY *is at the desk.*)

KIRBY. You see, I need something to relieve the daily nerve strain. After a week in Wall Street I'd go crazy if I didn't have something like that. Lot of men I know have yachts—just for that very reason.

GRANDPA. (*Mildly.*) Why don't they give up Wall Street?

KIRBY. How's that?

GRANDPA. I was just joking.

MRS. KIRBY. I think it's necessary for everyone to have a hobby. Of course, it's more to me than a hobby, but my great solace is— spiritualism.

PENNY. Spiritualism? Now, Mrs. Kirby, everybody knows that's a fake.

MRS. KIRBY. (*Freezing.*) To me, Mrs. Sycamore, spiritualism is— well—I would rather not discuss it, Mrs. Sycamore. (*She looks at* KIRBY. *He rises.*)

PAUL. (*Rising from couch and crossing to* PENNY.) Remember, Penny, you've got one or two hobbies of your own.

PENNY. Yes, but not silly ones.

53

GRANDPA. (*With a little cough.*) I don't think it matters what the hobby is—the important thing is to have one.

KOL. (*Crossing over back of table to* D.L., *in front of desk.*) To be ideal, a hobby should improve the body as well as the mind. The Romans were a great people! Why? What was their hobby? Wrestling. In wrestling you have to think quick with the mind and act quick with the body.

KIRBY. Yes, but I'm afraid wrestling is not very practical for most of us. (*He gives a deprecating little laugh.*) I wouldn't make a very good showing as a wrestler.

KOL. You could be a *great* wrestler. You are built for it. Look! (*With a startlingly quick movement* KOLENKHOV *grabs* KIRBY'S *arms, knocks his legs from under him with a quick movement of a foot, and presto!* KIRBY *is flat on his whatsis. Not only that, but instantaneously* KOLENKHOV *is on top of him.* MRS. KIRBY *rises. Just at this moment* ALICE *re-enters the room—naturally, she stands petrified. Then rushes immediately to the rescue,* TONY *and* ED *arriving at the scene of battle first. Amidst the general confusion they help* KIRBY *to his feet.*)

ALICE. Mr. Kirby! Are you—hurt?

TONY. Are you all right, Father?

KIRBY. (*Pulling himself together.*) I—I—uh —— (*He blinks, uncertainly.*) Where are my glasses?

ALICE. Here they are, Mr. Kirby. . . . Oh, Mr. Kirby, they're broken. (PAUL *turns to* PENNY.)

KOL. (*Full of apology.*) Oh, I am sorry. But when you wrestle again, Mr. Kirby, you will of course not wear glasses!

KIRBY. (*Coldly furious.*) I do not intend to wrestle again, Mr. Kolenkhov. (*He draws himself up, stiffly, and in return gets a sharp pain in the back. He gives a little gasp.*)

TONY. (*He assists his father to chair* L. *of table.*) Better sit down, Father.

ALICE. (*Crossing to* KOLENKHOV.) Mr. Kolenkhov, how could you do such a thing? Why didn't somebody stop him? (KOLENKHOV *turns* U.S.)

MRS. KIRBY. (*Rises.*) I think, if you don't mind, perhaps we had better be going. (*Gathers wraps.*) (GRANDPA *rises.*)

TONY. Mother!

ALICE. (*Close to tears.*) Oh, Mrs. Kirby—please! Please don't go! Mr. Kirby—please! I—I've ordered some scrambled eggs for you, and—plain salad —— Oh, please don't go!

KOL. (*Comes* D.L.) I am sorry if I did something wrong. And I apologize. (*Crosses* U.L.)

ALICE. I can't tell you how sorry I am, Mr. Kirby. If I'd been here ———

KIRBY. (*From a great height.*) That's quite all right.

TONY. Of course it is. It's all right, Alice. (*To* MRS. KIRBY.) We're not going. (*Arm around* ALICE.)

(*A moment's silence—no one knows quite what to say. Then* MRS. KIRBY *looks at* KIRBY *and sits. Then* KIRBY *sits. Finally* GRANDPA *sits.*)

PENNY. (*Brightly.*) Well! That was exciting for a minute, wasn't it?

GRANDPA. (*Quickly.*) You were talking about your orchids, Mr. Kirby. Do you raise many different varieties?

KIRBY. (*Still unbending.*) I'm afraid I've quite forgotten about my orchids. (*More silence, and everyone very uncomfortable.*)

ALICE. I'm—awfully sorry, Mr. Kirby.

KOL. (*Coming* D.L. *Exploding.*) What did I do that was so terrible? I threw him on the floor! Did it kill him?

ALICE. Please, Mr. Kolenkhov. (*An annoyed gesture from* KOLENKHOV. *He sits in desk chair. Another general pause.*)

PENNY. I'm sure dinner won't be any time at all now. (*Crosses* U.R., *looks off into kitchen. A pained smile from* MRS. KIRBY.)

ESSIE. (*Coming* D.S.R.) Would you like some candy while you're waiting, Mr. Kirby? I've got some freshly made.

KIRBY. My doctor does not permit me to eat candy. Thank you.

ESSIE. But these are nothing, Mr. Kirby. Just cocoanut and marshmallow and fudge.

ALICE. Don't, Essie.

ESSIE. Well —— (*Crosses to couch. They sit there again.*) (*Then* RHEBA *appears in kitchen doorway, beckoning violently to* ALICE.)

RHEBA. (*In a loud whisper.*) Miss Alice! Miss Alice!

ALICE. Excuse me. (*Starts* U.R.) What is it, Rheba? (*Quickly flies to* RHEBA'S *side.*)

RHEBA. The eggs done fell down the sink.

ALICE. (*Desperately.*) Make some more! Quick!

RHEBA. I ain't got any.

ALICE. Send Donald out for some!

RHEBA. (*Disappearing* U.R.) All right.

ALICE. (*Calling after her.*) Tell him to hurry! (*She turns back to the* KIRBYS.) I'm so sorry. There'll be a little delay, but everything will be ready in just a minute. (*At this moment* DONALD *fairly shoots out of kitchen door and across living room, beating the Olympic record for all time. SLAM on* DONALD'S *exit. He exits through hall door* U.L. PENNY *tries to ease situation with a gay little laugh. It doesn't quite come off, however.*) "Woosh!"

TONY. I've certainly put you people to a lot of trouble, with my stupidity.

GRANDPA. Not at all, Tony.

PENNY. (*Coming down* R. *of table.*) Look! Why don't we all play a game of some sort while we're waiting?

TONY. Oh, that'd be fine.

ALICE. Mother, I don't think Mr. and Mrs. Kirby ——

KOL. (*Rising from desk chair.*) *I* have an idea. I know a wonderful trick with a glass of water. (*He reaches for a full glass that stands on desk. Crosses to* KIRBY *and holds it over* KIRBY'S *head.*)

ALICE. (*Quickly.*) No, Mr. Kolenkhov.

GRANDPA. (*Rises, shaking his head.*) No-o, Mr. Kolenkhov. (*Sits.*) (*A shrug and* KOLENKHOV *returns glass to desk.*)

PENNY. But I'm sure Mr. and Mrs. Kirby would love this game. It's perfectly harmless.

ALICE. Please, Mother . . .

KIRBY. I'm not very good at games, Mrs. Sycamore.

PENNY. (*Crossing below table to the desk.*) Oh, but *any* fool could play this game, Mr. Kirby. All you do is write your name on a piece of paper —— (*Getting pads and pencils.*) (TONY *helps* KOLENKHOV *and himself to pads and pencils.*)

ALICE. But, mother, Mr. Kirby doesn't want ——

PENNY. Oh, he'll love it! (*Going right on distributing pencils, pads.*) Here you are, Mr. Kirby. Write your name on this piece of paper. And Mrs. Kirby, you do the same on this one. (PAUL, ESSIE *and* ED *sit on couch.* ESSIE *takes pencils,* ED *pads.*)

ALICE. Mother, what *is* this game?

PENNY. (*Crossing back of table to* L. KOLENKHOV *sits at desk.*) I used to play it at school. It's called Forget-Me-Not. Here you are, Grandpa. Now, I'm going to call out five words—just anything at all—and as I say each word, you're to put down the first thing that comes into your mind. Is that clear? For instance, if I say "grass," you might put down "green"—just whatever you think of, see? Or if I call out "chair," you might put down "table." It shows the re-

56

actions people have to different things. You see how simple it is, Mr. Kirby?

TONY. Come on, Father! Be a sport!

KIRBY. (*Stiffly.*) Very well. I shall be happy to play it.

PENNY. You see, Alice? He *does* want to play.

ALICE. (*Uneasily.*) Well ——

PENNY. Now, then! Are we ready?

KOL. Ready!

PENNY. Now, remember—you must play fair. Put down the first thing that comes into your mind.

KIRBY. (*Pencil poised.*) I understand.

PENNY. Everybody ready? . . . The first word is "potatoes." (*She repeats it.*) "Potatoes." . . . Ready for the next one? . . . "Bathroom." (ALICE *shifts rather uneasily.*)

ALICE. Mother! (*But seeing that no one else seems to mind, she relaxes again.*)

PENNY. Bathroom!—Got that?

KOL. Go ahead.

PENNY. All ready? . . . "Lust."

ALICE. Mother, this is not exactly what you ——

PENNY. Nonsense, Alice—that word's all right.

ALICE. Mother, it's *not* all right.

MRS. KIRBY. (*Unexpectedly.*) Oh, I don't know. (*To* ALICE.) It seems to me that's a perfectly fair word.

PENNY. (*To* ALICE.) You see? Now, you mustn't interrupt the game. (ALICE *drifts* U.S.)

KIRBY. May I have that last word again, please?

PENNY. "Lust," Mr. Kirby.

KIRBY. (*Writing.*) I've got it.

GRANDPA. This is quite a game, isn't it?

PENNY. Sssh, Grandpa. . . . All ready? . . . "Honeymoon." (ESSIE *snickers a little, which is all it takes to start* PENNY *off. Then she suddenly remembers herself.*) Now, Essie! . . . All right. The last word is "Sex."

ALICE. (*Under her breath.*) Mother! (*Crossing to buffet.*)

PENNY. Everybody got "sex"? . . . All right— (*She takes* TONY'S *and* KOLENKHOV'S *papers.*) now give me all the papers. May I have your paper, Mr. Kirby? (*Crosses back of table to* R. *gathering the pads.*) (*Three at table tear off sheets.* ED *hands three pads to* PENNY.)

GRANDPA. What happens now?

PENNY. Oh, this is the best part. Now I read out your reactions. (*Coming* D.R.)

KIRBY. I see. It's really quite an interesting game.

PENNY. I knew you'd like it. I'll read your paper first, Mr. Kirby. (*To the others.*) I'm going to read Mr. Kirby's paper first. Listen, everybody! This is Mr. Kirby. . . . "Potatoes—steak." That's very good. See how they go together? Steak and potatoes?

KIRBY. (*Modestly, but obviously pleased with himself.*) I just happened to think of it. (ALICE *turns front.*)

PENNY. It's *very* good. . . . "Bathroom—toothpaste." Well! "Lust—unlawful." Isn't that nice? "Honeymoon—trip." Yes. (*Giggle.*) And "sex—male." Oh yes, of course . . . you are. That's really a wonderful paper, Mr. Kirby.

KIRBY. (*Taking a curtain call.*) Thank you. . . . It's more than just a game, you know. It's sort of an experiment in psychology, isn't it?

PENNY. Yes, it is—it shows just how your *mind* works. Now we'll see how *Mrs.* Kirby's mind works. . . . Ready? . . . This is *Mrs.* Kirby. . . . "Potatoes—starch." I know just what you mean, Mrs. Kirby. M-m—oh dear! . . . "Bathroom—Mr. Kirby."

KIRBY. What's that?

PENNY. "Bathroom—Mr. Kirby."

KIRBY. (*Turning to his wife.*) I don't quite *follow that,* my dear.

MRS. KIRBY. I don't know—I just thought of you in connection with it. After all, you *are* in there a good deal, Anthony. Bathing, and shaving—well, you *do* take a long time.

KIRBY. Indeed? I hadn't realized that I was being selfish in the matter. . . . Go on, Mrs. Sycamore.

ALICE. (*Worried. Comes down to* KIRBY.) I think it's a very silly game and we ought to stop it.

MRS. KIRBY. Yes.

KIRBY. No, no. Please go on, Mrs. Sycamore. (ALICE *crosses up.*)

PENNY. Where was I? . . . Oh, yes. . . . "Lust—human."

KIRBY. Human? (*Thin-lipped.*) Really! Miriam!

MRS. KIRBY. I just meant, Anthony, that lust is after all a—human emotion.

KIRBY. I don't agree with you, Miriam. Lust is *not* a *human* emotion. It is depraved.

MRS. KIRBY. Very well, Anthony. I'm wrong.

ALICE. (*Crossing down to* L. *of* KIRBY.) Really, it's the most pointless game. Suppose we play Twenty Questions?

MRS. KIRBY. Yes.

KIRBY. (*Raises hand.* ALICE *goes* U.S.) No, I find *this* game rather interesting. Will you go on, Mrs. Sycamore? What was the next word?

PENNY. (*Reluctantly.*) Honeymoon.

KIRBY. Oh, yes. And what was Mrs. Kirby's answer?

PENNY. Ah—"Honeymoon—dull."

KIRBY. (*Murderously calm.*) Did you say—dull?

MRS. KIRBY. What I meant, Anthony, was that Hot Springs was not very gay that season. All those old people sitting on the porch all afternoon, and—nothing to do at night. (*Realizes she has gone too far.*)

KIRBY. That was not your reaction at the time, as I recall it.

TONY. (*Crosses in a step.*) Father, this is only a *game*.

KIRBY. A very illuminating game. Go on, Mrs. Sycamore!

PENNY. (*Brightly, having taken a look ahead.*) This one's all right, Mr. Kirby. "Sex—Wall Street."

KIRBY. Wall Street? What do you mean by that, Miriam?

MRS. KIRBY. (*Nervously.*) I don't know what I meant, Anthony. Nothing.

KIRBY. But you must have meant something, Miriam, or you wouldn't have put it down.

MRS. KIRBY. It was just the first thing that came into my head, that's all.

KIRBY. But what does it mean? Sex—Wall Street.

MRS. KIRBY. (*Annoyed.*) Oh, I don't know what it means, Anthony. It's just that you're always talking about Wall Street, even when —— (*She catches herself.*) I don't know what I meant. . . . Would you mind terribly, Alice, if we didn't stay for dinner? (*Rises.* GRANDPA *and* KOLENKHOV *rise. Also* ESSIE, ED *and* PAUL.) I'm afraid this game has given me a headache.

ALICE. (*Quietly.*) I understand, Mrs. Kirby.

KIRBY. (*Rises. Clearing his throat.*) Yes, possibly we'd better postpone the dinner, if you don't mind. (KOLENKHOV *drifts* U.C.)

PENNY. But you're coming tomorrow night, aren't you?

MRS. KIRBY. (*Quickly.*) I'm afraid we have an engagement tomorrow night. (*Wrap is half on shoulders.*)

KIRBY. Perhaps we'd better postpone the whole affair a little while. The hot weather and—ah ——

TONY.. (*Smouldering.*) I think we're being very ungracious, Father. Of *course* we'll stay to dinner—tonight.

MRS. KIRBY. (*Unyielding.*) I have a very bad headache, Tony.

KIRBY. (*To* TONY.) Come, come, Tony, I'm sure everyone understands. (KOLENKHOV *continues drifting down to back of the table.*)

TONY. (*Flaring.*) Well, *I* don't. I think we ought to stay.

ALICE. (*Very low. She comes down to* TONY.) No, Tony.

TONY. What?

ALICE. We were fools, Tony, ever to think it would work. It won't. Mr. Kirby, I won't be at the office tomorrow. I—won't be there at all any more. (*Crosses* D.L. *below desk.*)

TONY. (*Follows her. Puts his arm around her.*) Alice, what are you talking about?

KIRBY. (*To* ALICE.) I'm sorry, my dear—very sorry. . . . Are you ready, Miriam?

MRS. KIRBY. (*With enormous dignity. She crosses over to* KIRBY.) Yes, Anthony.

TONY. Darling, you mustn't mind this.

KIRBY. Oh—it's been very nice to have met you all. (*With* MRS. KIRBY, *he goes as far as the archway.*)

MRS. KIRBY. Yes, lovely.

KIRBY. Are you coming, Tony?

TONY. No, Father. I'm not.

KIRBY. (*Crossing up to arch with* MRS. KIRBY.) I see. . . . Your mother and I will be waiting for you at home. . . . Good night.

PENNIE and ESSIE. Good night.

(*Before the* KIRBYS *can take more than a step toward the door, however, a new* FIGURE *looms up in the archway. It is a quiet and competent-looking individual with a steely eye, and two more just like him loom up behind him.*)

THE MAN. (*Very quietly.*) Stay right where you are, everybody. (*There is a little scream from* MRS. KIRBY, *an exclamation from* PENNY.) Don't move.

PENNY. Oh, good heavens!

KIRBY. (*Speaks on cue "Don't move."*) How dare you? Why, what does this mean?

GRANDPA. What is all this?

KIRBY. I demand an explanation!

THE MAN. Keep your mouth shut, you! (PENNY *turns to* PAUL. ED *backs up as G-Man crosses* R. *He advances slowly into the room, looking the group over. Then he turns to one of his men.*) Which one is it?

THIRD MAN. (*Goes over and puts a hand on* ED'S *shoulder and brings him* D.R. ESSIE *follows.*) This is him.

ED. Heh! What are you doing?

ESSIE. Ed!

ED. (*Terrified.*) Why, what do you mean?

ALICE. (*Crossing to* GRANDPA.) Grandpa, what is it?

KIRBY. This is an outrage!

THE MAN. Shut up! (*He turns to* ED.) What's your name?

ED. Edward—Carmichael. I haven't done anything.

THE MAN. You haven't, huh?

GRANDPA. (*Not at all scared.*) This seems rather high-handed to me. What's it all about?

THE MAN. Department of Justice.

PENNY. Oh, my goodness! J-men!

ESSIE. Ed, what have you done?

ED. I haven't done anything.

GRANDPA. What's the boy done, Officer?

ALICE. What is it? What's it all about?

THE MAN. (*Taking his time, and surveying the room.*) That door lead to the cellar?

PENNY. Yes it does.

PAUL. Yes.

THE MAN. (*Ordering a man to investigate.*) Mac . . . (THIRD G-MAN *exits* D.R.) . . . Jim!

JIM. Yes, sir.

THE MAN. Take a look *upstairs* and see what you find.

JIM. Okay. (JIM *exits upstairs.*)

ED. (*Panicky.*) I haven't done anything.

THE MAN. Come here, you! (*He takes some slips of paper out of his pocket.*) Ever see these before?

ED. (*Gulping.*) They're my—circulars.

THE MAN. You print this stuff, huh?

ED. Yes, sir.

THE MAN. And you put 'em into boxes of candy to get 'em into people's homes.

ESSIE. The Love Dreams!

ED. Bu. I didn't mean anything ——

THE MAN. You didn't, huh? (*He reads circulars.*) "Dynamite the

Capitol!" "Dynamite the White House!" "Dynamite the Supreme
Court!" "God is the State; the State is God!"

ED. But I didn't mean that. I just like to print. Don't I, Grandpa?
(DONALD *enters* U.L.)

GRANDPA. (*Waves* ED *and* ESSIE U.S.) Now, Officer, the Government's in no danger from Ed. Printing is just his hobby, that's all.
He prints anything.

THE MAN. He does, eh?

PENNY. I never heard of such nonsense.

KIRBY. I refuse to stay here and ———

(DE PINNA, *at this point, is shoved through cellar door by* MAC, *pro-
testing as he comes.*)

DE PINNA. Hey, let me get my pipe, will you? Let me get my pipe!

MAC. Shut up, you! . . . We were right, Chief. They've got enough
gunpowder down there to blow up the whole city.

PAUL. But we only use that ———

THE MAN. Keep still! . . . Everybody in this house is under arrest.

KIRBY. What's that?

MRS. KIRBY. Oh, good heavens!

GRANDPA. Now look here, Officer—this is all nonsense.

DE PINNA. You'd better let me get my pipe. I left it ———

THE MAN. Shut up, all of you!

KOL. It seems to me, Officer ———

THE MAN. Shut up! (*From the stairs comes sound of drunken singing—"There was a young lady," etc.* GAY, *wrapped in* PENNY'S
*negligee, is being carried down stairway by a somewhat bewildered
G-man.*)

JIM. Keep still, you! Stop that! Stop it!

THE MAN. Who's that?

GRANDPA. That is my mother! (*He sits.*)

KOL. The fireworks! The fireworks! (*And then we hear from the
cellar. A whole year's supply of fireworks just goes off.*)

RHEBA. (*Enters* U.R.) Donald! Donald!

(MRS. KIRBY'S *scream is just a little louder than the explosion.*)

KIRBY. Miriam! Miriam! Are you all right? Are you all right?

TONY. (*Dashing to his mother.*) It's all right! Mother! There's no
danger.

ALICE. Grandpa! Grandpa! (*Crosses to* GRANDPA.)

GRANDPA. (*Ever so quietly.*) Well, well, well!

62

DE PINNA. (*Wrenching himself loose from the G-man.*) Let go of me! I've got to go down there!

PAUL. Good lord! (*With* DE PINNA, *he dashes into the cellar.*)

PENNY. My manuscripts! I've got to save my manuscripts! (*She dashes to her desk.*)

ED. My xylophone! How will I get the xylophone out?

ESSIE. Mr. Kolenkhov! Mr. Kolenkhov!

KOL. Do not worry! Do not worry!

DONALD. (*Rushing toward the kitchen.*) It's all right, Rheba, it's all right!

THE G-MAN. (*Vainly trying to keep order.*) Line up, you people! Line up, all of you!

(*And* GAY *just keeps singing.*)

CURTAIN

ACT III

The following day. RHEBA *is in the midst of setting table for dinner, pausing occasionally in her labors to listen to the Edwin C. Hill of the moment*—DONALD. *With intense interest and concentration, he is reading aloud from a newspaper.*

DONALD. ". . . for appearance in the West Side Court this morning. After spending the night in jail, the defendants, thirteen in all, were brought before Judge Callahan and given suspended sentences for manufacturing fireworks without a permit."

RHEBA. (*Puts plate down.*) Yah. Kept me in the same cell with a strip teaser from a burlesque show.

DONALD. I was in the cell with Mr. Kirby. My, he was mad!

RHEBA. (*Sets knife and fork.*) Mrs. Kirby and the strip teaser—they were fighting *all night.*

DONALD. Whole lot about *Mr.* Kirby here. (RHEBA *places napkins. Reading again.*) "Anthony W. Kirby, head of Kirby & Co., 62 Wall Street, who was among those apprehended, declared he was in no way interested in the manufacture of fireworks, but refused to state why he was on the premises at the time of the raid. Mr. Kirby is a member of the Union Club, the Racquet Club, the Harvard Club, and the National Geographic Society." My, he certainly is a joiner!

RHEBA. (*Pushes in chair above table.*) All them rich men are Elks or something.

DONALD. (*Looking up from his paper.*) I suppose, after all this, Mr. Tony ain't ever going to marry Miss Alice, huh?

RHEBA. No, suh, and it's too bad, too. Miss Alice sure *loves* that boy.

DONALD. Ever notice how white folks always getting themselves in trouble?

RHEBA. Yassuh, I'm glad I'm colored.

DONALD. Me, too.

RHEBA. (*She sighs heavily. Turns chair* L. *in.*) I don't know what I'm going to do with all that food out in the kitchen. Ain't going to be no party tonight, that's sure.

DONALD. Ain't we going to eat it anyhow?

RHEBA. (*Gets salad plates from buffet.*) Well, I'm cooking it, but I don't think anybody going to have an appetite.

DONALD. *I'm* hungry.

RHEBA. (*Setting salad forks.*) Well, *they ain't.* They're all so broke up about Miss Alice.

DONALD. What's she want to go 'way for? Where's she going?

RHEBA. (*Puts half of salad plates* D.S. *of table.*) I don't know— mountains some place. And she's *going,* all right, no matter what they say. I know Miss Alice when she gets that look in her eye.

DONALD. Too bad, ain't it?

RHEBA. Sure is.

(DE PINNA *comes up from cellar, bearing earmarks of the previous day's catastrophe. There is a small bandage around his head and over one eye, and another around his* R. *hand. He also limps slightly.*)

DE PINNA. Not even a balloon left. Look. (*Pointing to exploded firecracker he is holding.*)

RHEBA. How's your hand, Mr. De Pinna? Better?

DE PINNA. Yes, it's better. (*A step toward kitchen.*) Is there some more olive oil out there?

RHEBA. (*Nods.*) It's in the salad bowl.

DE PINNA. Thanks. (*Crosses to* R. *He goes out kitchen door as* PENNY *comes down stairs. It is a new and rather subdued* PENNY. DONALD *rises.* RHEBA *turns to her.*)

PENNY. (*With a sigh.*) Well, she's going. Nothing anybody said could change her.

RHEBA. She ain't going to stay away long, is she, Mrs. Sycamore?

PENNY. I don't know, Rheba. She won't say.

RHEBA. My, going to be lonesome around here without her. (*She goes into kitchen* U.R.)

DONALD. How *you* feel, Mrs. Sycamore?

PENNY. Oh, I'm all right, Donald. Just kind of upset. (*She is at her desk.*) Perhaps if I do some work maybe I'll feel better. (*Sits at her desk.*)

DONALD. Well, I won't bother you then, Mrs. Sycamore. (*He goes into kitchen* U.R.) (PENNY *leans back and sits staring straight ahead.* PAUL *comes slowly down stairs; stands surveying room a moment; sighs.*)

PAUL. (*Coming* D.S.) She's going, Penny.

PENNY. Yes. (*She is quiet for a moment; then she starts to weep, softly.*)

65

PAUL. (*Going to her.*) Now, now, Penny.

PENNY. I can't help it, Paul. Somehow I feel it's our fault.

PAUL. It's mine more than yours, Penny. All these years I've just been—going along, enjoying myself, when maybe I should have been thinking more about Alice.

PENNY. Don't say that, Paul. You've been a wonderful father. And husband, too.

PAUL. (*Crossing to* L. *of table.*) No, I haven't. Maybe if I'd gone ahead and been an architect—I don't know—something Alice could have been proud of. I felt that all last night, looking at Mr. Kirby.

PENNY. But we've been so happy, Paul.

PAUL. I know, but maybe that's not enough. I used to think it was, but—I'm kind of all mixed up now.

PENNY. (*After a pause.*) What time is she going?

PAUL. Pretty soon. Train leaves at half past seven.

PENNY. Oh, if only she'd see Tony. I'm sure he could persuade her.

PAUL. But she won't, Penny. He's been trying all day.

PENNY. Where is he now?

PAUL. (*Crossing below table to* R.) I don't know—I suppose walking around the block again. Anyhow, she won't talk to him.

PENNY. Maybe Tony can catch her as she's leaving.

PAUL. It won't help, Penny.

PENNY. No, I don't suppose so. . . . I feel so sorry for Tony, too. (GRANDPA *comes down stairs* L.—*unsmiling, but not too depressed by the situation.* PENNY, *anxiously, rises.*) Well?—Grandpa?

GRANDPA. Now, Penny, let the girl alone.

PENNY. But, Grandpa ——

GRANDPA. (*Crossing back of table to chair* R.) Suppose she *goes* to the Adirondacks? She'll be back. You can take just so much Adirondacks, and then you come home.

PENNY. (*Sits desk chair.*) Oh, but it's all so terrible, Grandpa.

GRANDPA. In a way, but it has its bright side, too. (*Sits* R. *of table.*)

PAUL. How do you mean?

GRANDPA. Well, Mr. Kirby getting into the patrol wagon, for one thing, and the expression on his face when he and Donald had to take a bath together. I'll never forget that if I live to be a hundred, and I warn you people I intend to. If I can have things like that going on.

PENNY. (*Rises—crosses to* L. *of table.*) Oh, it was even worse with Mrs. Kirby. When the matron stripped her. There was a burlesque dancer there and she kept singing a strip song while Mrs. Kirby undressed. (*She goes back to desk.*)

GRANDPA. I'll bet you Bar Harbor is going to seem pretty dull to the Kirbys this summer. (*With a determined step,* ALICE *comes swiftly down stairs. Over her arm she carries a couple of dresses. Looking neither to* R. *nor* L., *she heads for kitchen.*) Need any help, Alice? (ED *starts down stairs carrying suitcase and hatbox.*)

ALICE. (*In a strained voice.*) No thanks, Grandpa. I'm just going to press these.

PENNY. Alice, dear ——

GRANDPA. Now, Penny. (ED *has appeared in hallway with a hatbox, etc.,* ESSIE *behind him.*)

ED. (*Puts bags in hall.*) I'll bring the big bag down as soon as you're ready, Alice.

ALICE. Thank you.

ESSIE. Do you want to take some candy along for the train, Alice?

ALICE. No, thanks, Essie.

PENNY. (*Crossing step to* R.) Really, Alice, you could be just as alone here as you could in the mountains. You could stay right in your room all the time.

ALICE. (*Quietly.*) No, Mother, I want to be by myself—away from everybody. (*She includes the whole group. Crosses down to table —picks up a dart.*) I love you all—you know that. But I just have to go away for a while. I'll be all right. . . . Father, did you phone for a cab?

PAUL. No, I didn't know you wanted one.

PENNY. Oh, I told Mr. De Pinna to tell you, Paul. Didn't he tell you?

ED. Oh, he told *me,* but I forgot.

ALICE. (*The final straw.*) Oh, I wish I lived in a family that didn't always forget *everything.* That—that behaved the way *other* people's families do. I'm sick of corn flakes, and—Donald, and—oh—(*Unconsciously, in her impatience, is surprised to find dart suddenly in her hand.*)—everything! (*She dashes dart to floor.*) Why can't we be like other people? Roast beef, and two green vegetables, and—doilies on the table and—a place you could bring your friends to—without —— (*Unable to control herself further, she bursts out of room, into kitchen* U.R.)

ESSIE. I'll—see if I can do anything. (*She goes into kitchen* U.R.) (*The others look at each other for a moment, helplessly.* PENNY, *with a sigh, drops into her chair again.* PAUL *drifts* R. GRANDPA

67

mechanically picks up dart from floor; smooths out the feathers, sits. ED *crosses to xylophone with a futile gesture, runs his hammer idly over xylophone keys. He stops quickly as every head turns to look at him. The sound of the door opening, and* TONY *appears in archway. A worried and disheveled* TONY.)

PENNY. (*Rises quickly.*) Tony, talk to her! She's in the kitchen.

TONY. Thanks. (*He goes immediately into kitchen. The family, galvanized, listen intently. Almost immediately* ALICE *emerges from kitchen again, followed by* TONY. *She crosses living-room and starts quickly up stairs.*) Alice, won't you listen to me? Please!

ALICE. (*Not stopping.*) Tony, it's no use.

TONY. (*Following her.*) Alice, you're not being fair. At least let me talk to you. (*They are both gone—up the stairs.*) (ESSIE *comes out of kitchen.*)

ESSIE. Where'd they go?

(ED, *with a gesture, indicates upstairs region.*)

ED. Upstairs.

ESSIE. (*Looking upstairs.*) She walked right out the minute he came in. (PENNY *sits at desk.* ESSIE *sits* L. *of table as* DE PINNA *also emerges from kitchen* U.R.)

DE PINNA. (*Crossing down to* GRANDPA.) Knocked the olive oil right out of my hand. I'm going to smell kind of fishy.

GRANDPA. How're you feeling, Mr. De Pinna? Hand still hurting you?

DE PINNA. No, it's better.

PAUL. Everything burnt up, huh? Downstairs?

DE PINNA. (*Nodding, sadly.*) Everything. And my Roman costume, too.

GRANDPA. (*To* PENNY.) M-m-m. I told you there was a bright side to everything. All except my twenty-three years' back income tax. (*He pulls an envelope out of his pocket.*) I get another letter every day.

DE PINNA. Say, what are you going to do about that, Grandpa?

GRANDPA. Well, I had a kind of idea yesterday. It may not work, (KOLENKHOV *starts on from* U.L. *door.*) but I'm trying it, anyhow.

DE PINNA. (*Eagerly.*) What is it?

(*Suddenly* KOLENKHOV *appears in the arch* U.L.)

KOL. Good evening, everybody!

68

PENNY. Why, Mr. Kolenkhov!

GRANDPA. Hello, Kolenkhov.

KOL. Forgive me. The door was open.

GRANDPA. Come on in.

KOL. (*Comes into room.*) You will excuse my coming today. I realize you are—upset.

PENNY. That's all right, Mr. Kolenkhov.

ESSIE. I don't think I can take a lesson, Mr. Kolenkhov. I don't feel up to it.

KOL. (*Uncertainly.*) Well, I—ah ——

PENNY. Oh, but do stay to dinner, Mr. Kolenkhov. We've got all that food out there, and somebody's got to eat it.

KOL. I will be happy to, Madame Sycamore.

PENNY. Fine.

KOL. Thank you. . . . Now, I wonder if I know you well enough to ask of you a great favor.

PENNY. Why, of course, Mr. Kolenkhov. What is it?

KOL. (*Comes D.S.*) You have heard me talk about my friend, the Grand Duchess Olga Katrina.

PENNY. Yes?

KOL. She is a great woman, the Grand Duchess. (*To group.*) Her cousin was the Czar of Russia, and today she is a waitress in Childs' Restaurant, Times Square.

PENNY. Yes, I know. If there's anything at all that we can do, Mr. Kolenkhov . . .

KOL. I tell you. The Grand Duchess Olga Katrina has not had a good meal since before the Revolution.

GRANDPA. She must be hungry.

KOL. And today the Grand Duchess not only has her day off— Thursday—but it is also the anniversary of Peter the Great. A remarkable man!

PENNY. (*Rises.*) Mr. Kolenkhov, if you mean you'd like the Grand Duchess to come to dinner, why, we'd be honored.

ESSIE. (*Rises.*) Oh, yes!

KOL. (*With a bow.*) In the name of the Grand Duchess, I thank you. (*Starts for door.*)

PENNY. I can hardly wait to meet her. Where is she now?

KOL. She is outside in the street, waiting. I bring her in. (*And he goes out* U.L. DE PINNA *rushes to the cellar door for his coat off stage.*)

PENNY. (*Feverishly.*) Ed, straighten your tie. Essie, your dress. How do *I* look? All right?

(KOLENKHOV *appears in hallway and stands at rigid attention.*)

GRANDPA. You know, if this keeps on I want to live to be a hundred and *fifty.*

KOL. (*His voice booming.*) The Grand Duchess Olga Katrina! (*And* GRAND DUCHESS OLGA KATRINA, *wheat cakes and maple syrup out of her life for the day, sweeps into the room. She wears a dinner gown that has seen better days, and the whole is surmounted by an extremely tacky-looking evening wrap, trimmed with bits of ancient and moth-eaten fur. But once a Grand Duchess, always a Grand Duchess. She rises above everything—Childs, evening wrap, and all.*) Your Highness, permit me to present Madame Sycamore —(PENNY, *having seen a movie or two in her time, knows just what to do. She curtsies right to the floor, and catches hold of a chair just in time.*) Madame Carmichael—(ESSIE *does a curtsy that begins where all others leave off. Starting on her toes, she merges "The Dying Swan" with an extremely elaborate genuflection.*) Grandpa

———

GRANDPA. (*With a little bow.*) Madame.

KOL. Mr. Carmichael, Mr. Sycamore, and Mr. De Pinna.

(PAUL *and* ED *content themselves with courteous little bows, but not so the social-minded* DE PINNA. *He curtsies to the floor—and stays there for a moment.*)

GRANDPA. All right now, Mr. De Pinna.

(DE PINNA *gets to his feet again.* ESSIE *crosses down to chair* L. *of table.*)

PENNY. Will you be seated, Your Highness?

GRAND DUCHESS. (*Sits* L. *of table.*) Thank you. You are most kind. (GRANDPA *sits.*)

PENNY. (ESSIE *sits above table.*) We are honored to receive you, Your Highness. (*Backing away.*)

GRAND DUCHESS. I am most happy to be here. How soon is dinner? (*To* PENNY.)

PENNY. (*A little startled.*) Oh, it'll be quite soon, Your Highness —very soon.

GRAND DUCHESS. I do not mean to be rude, but I must be back at the restaurant by eight o'clock. I am substituting for another waitress.

KOL. I will make sure you are on time, Your Highness.

GRAND DUCHESS. Thank you, Kolenkhov.

DE PINNA. You know, Highness, I think you *waited on me* in Childs' once. The Seventy-second Street place?

GRAND DUCHESS. No, no. That was my sister.

KOL. The Grand Duchess Natasha.

GRAND DUCHESS. *I* work in Times Square.

DE PINNA. Oh!

GRANDPA. Quite a lot of your folks living over here now, aren't there?

GRAND DUCHESS. (*To* GRANDPA.) Oh, yes—many. (*Front.*) My uncle, the Grand Duke Sergei—he is an *elevator man* at Macy's. A very nice man. (*To* GRANDPA.) Then there is my cousin, Prince Alexis. He will not speak to the rest of us because he works at Hattie Carnegie. He is in ladies' underwear.

KOL. When he was selling hot dogs at Coney Island he was willing to talk to you.

GRAND DUCHESS. Ah, Kolenkhov, our time is coming. My sister, Natasha, is studying to be a manicurist, Uncle Sergei they have promised to make floorwalker, and next month I get transferred to the *Fifth Avenue* Childs'. From there it is only a step to *Schrafft's',* and (*To* GRANDPA.) *then* we will see what Prince Alexis says!

GRANDPA. (*Nodding.*) I think you've got him.

GRAND DUCHESS. You are telling *me?* (*She laughs in a triumphant Russian laugh, in which* KOLENKHOV *joins.*)

PENNY. Your Highness—did you know the Czar? Personally, I mean.

GRAND DUCHESS. Of course—he was my cousin. It was terrible, what happened, but perhaps it was for the best. Where could he get a job now?

KOL. Pravda, Pravda. That is true.

GRAND DUCHESS. (*Philosophically.*) And poor relations are poor relations. It is the same in every family. My cousin, the King of Sweden—he was very nice to us for about ten years. Every once in a while he would send a money order. But then he said, (*To* GRANDPA.) I just cannot go on. I am not doing so well myself. I do not blame him.

PENNY. No, of course not. . . . Would you excuse me for just a moment? (*She goes to foot of stairs and stands peering up anxiously, hoping for news of* ALICE.)

DE PINNA. (*The historian at heart. Crosses in a step.*) Tell me, Grand Duchess, is it true what they say about Rasputin?

GRAND DUCHESS. Everyone wants to know about Rasputin. . . . Yes, my dear sir, it is true. And how.

DE PINNA. You don't say?

KOL. Your Highness, we have to watch the time.

GRAND DUCHESS. Yes, I must not be late. The manager does not like me. He is a Communist. (*To* PENNY.)

PENNY. We'll hurry things up. Essie, why don't you go out in the kitchen and see if you can help Rheba? (DE PINNA *crossing* D.R. PAUL *drifts* U.S.)

GRAND DUCHESS. (*Rising.* ESSIE *and* GRANDPA *also rise,* ED *backs* U.S.) I will help, too. I am a very good cook.

PENNY. Oh, but Your Highness! Not on your day off!

GRAND DUCHESS. I do not mind. (*Front turn.*) Where is your kitchen? (KOLENKHOV *takes her wrap to hatrack.*)

ESSIE. Right through here, but you're the guest of honor, Your Highness.

GRAND DUCHESS. But I love to cook! Come, Kolenkhov! (*Beckons to* KOLENKHOV.) If they have got sour cream and pot-cheese I will make you some blintzes! (*And sweeps through kitchen door.*)

KOL. Ah! Blintzes! . . . Come, Pavlowa! We show you something! (*With* ESSIE, *he goes into the kitchen.*)

DE PINNA. Say! The Duchess is all right, isn't she? Hey, Duchess! Can I help? (*And into the kitchen.*)

ED. Gee! She's got a wonderful face for a mask, hasn't she?

PENNY. Really, she's a very nice woman, you know. Considering she's a Grand Duchess.

GRANDPA. Wonderful what some people go through, isn't it? And still keep kind of gay, too.

PENNY. M-m. She made me forget about everything for a minute. (*She returns to stairs and stands listening.*)

PAUL. I'd better call that cab, I suppose.

PENNY. No, wait, Paul. Here they are. Maybe Tony has —— (*She stops as* ALICE'S *step is heard on stair. She enters—dressed for traveling.* TONY *looms up behind her.*)

ALICE. (*Crossing to above table.*) Ed, will you go up and bring my bag down?

TONY. (*Quickly.*) Don't you do it, Ed! (ED *hesitates, uncertain.*)

ALICE. Ed, please!

TONY. (*A moment's pause; then he gives up.*) All right, Ed. Bring it down. (ED *goes up stairs.*) Do you know that you've got the stubbornest daughter in all forty-eight states? (*The doorbell rings.*)

ALICE. That must be the cab. (*She goes to door.*) (TONY *crosses to* U.C. PAUL *crosses to* R.)

GRANDPA. If it is, it's certainly wonderful service.

(*To the considerable surprise of everyone, the voice of* KIRBY *is heard at the front door.* GRANDPA *rises, goes to back of his chair.*)

KIRBY. Is Tony here, Alice?

ALICE. (*At* R. *of arch.*) Yes. Yes, he is. Come in, Mr. Kirby. (KIRBY *comes in.*)

GRANDPA. How do you do?

KIRBY. (*Uncomfortably.*) Ah—good evening.

PENNY. Good evening.

KIRBY. Forgive my intruding. . . . Tony, I want you to come home with me. Your mother is very upset.

TONY. (*He looks at* ALICE.) Very well, Father. . . . Good-bye, Alice.

ALICE. (*Very low.*) Good-bye, Tony.

KIRBY. (*Trying to ease the situation.*) I need hardly say that this is as painful to Mrs. Kirby and myself as it is to you people. I—I'm sorry, but I'm sure you understand.

GRANDPA. (*Coming down to table.*) Well, yes—and in a way, no. Now, I'm not the kind of person tries to run other people's lives, but the fact is, Mr. Kirby, I don't think these two young people have got as much sense as—ah—you and I have.

ALICE. (*Tense.*) Grandpa, will you please not do this?

GRANDPA. (*Disarmingly.*) I'm just talking to Mr. Kirby. A cat can look at a king, can't he? (ALICE, *with no further words, takes up phone and dials. There is finality in her every movement.*)

PENNY. You—you want me to do that for you, Alice?

ALICE. No, thanks, Mother.

PAUL. (*Looks at* PENNY.) You've got quite a while before the train goes, Alice.

ALICE. (*Into phone.*) Will you send a cab to 761 Claremont, right away, please? . . . That's right. Thank you. (*She hangs up. Starts* R.)

PAUL. Alice!

ALICE. (*Embrace.*) Father!

KIRBY. Are you ready, Tony?

GRANDPA. Mr. Kirby, I suppose after last night you think this family is kind of crazy?

KIRBY. No, I would not say that, although I am not accustomed to going out to dinner and spending the night in jail.

GRANDPA. Well, you've got to remember, Mr. Kirby, you came on the wrong night. Now tonight, I'll bet you, nothing'll happen at all. Maybe. (*Coming down* R. *of his chair.*)

KIRBY. (*Crossing to table.*) Mr. Vanderhof, it was not merely last night that convinced Mrs. Kirby and myself that this engagement would be unwise.

TONY. Father, I can handle my own affairs. (*He crosses to* ALICE *stage* R.) Alice, for the last time, will you marry me?

ALICE. No, Tony. I know exactly what your father means, and he's right.

TONY. No, he's *not,* Alice.

GRANDPA. (*Crosses to them.*) Alice, you're in love with this boy, and you're not marrying him because we're the kind of people we are.

ALICE. Grandpa ——

GRANDPA. I know. You think the two families wouldn't get along. Well, maybe they wouldn't—but who says they're right and we're wrong?

ALICE. I didn't say that, Grandpa. I only feel ——

GRANDPA. Well, what *I* feel is that Tony's too nice a boy to wake up twenty years from now with nothing in his life but stocks and bonds. (ALICE *and* TONY *drift upstage.*)

KIRBY. How's that?

GRANDPA. (*Turning to* KIRBY *and crossing to below table.*) Yes. Mixed up and unhappy, the way you are.

KIRBY. (*Outraged.*) I beg your pardon, Mr. Vanderhof. I am a very happy man. (ALICE *crosses to printing press.*)

GRANDPA. Are you?

KIRBY. Certainly I am.

GRANDPA. (*Sits.*) I don't think so. What do you think you get your indigestion from? Happiness? No, sir. You get it because most of your time is spent in doing things you don't want to do.

KIRBY. I don't do anything I don't want to do.

GRANDPA. Yes, you do. You said last night that at the end of a week in Wall Street you're pretty near crazy. Why do you keep on doing it?

KIRBY. Why do I keep on—why, that's my *business*. A man can't give up his business.

GRANDPA. Why not? You've got all the money you need. You can't take it with you.

KIRBY. That's a very easy thing to say, Mr. Vanderhof. But I have spent my entire life building up my business.

GRANDPA. And what's it got you? Same kind of mail every morning, same kind of deals, same kind of meetings, same dinners at night, same indigestion. Where does the fun come in? Don't you think there ought to be something *more,* Mr. Kirby? You must have wanted more than that when you started out. We haven't got too much time, you know—any of us.

KIRBY. What do you expect me to do? Live the way *you* do? Do nothing?

GRANDPA. Well, I have a lot of fun. Time enough for everything— read, talk, visit the zoo now and then, practice my darts, even have time to notice when spring comes around. Don't see anybody I don't want to, don't have six hours of things I *have* to do every day before I get *one* hour to do what I like in—and I haven't taken bicarbonate of soda in thirty-five years. What's the matter with that?

KIRBY. The matter with that? Suppose we *all* did it? A fine world we'd have, everybody going to *zoos.* Don't be ridiculous, Mr. Vanderhof. Who would do the work?

GRANDPA. There's always people that like to work—you can't *stop* them. Inventions, and they fly the ocean. There're always people to go down to Wall Street, too—because they *like* it. But from what I've seen of you I don't think you're one of them. I think you're missing something.

KIRBY. (*Crossing toward* PENNY.) I am not aware of missing anything.

GRANDPA. I wasn't either, till I quit. I used to get down to that office nine o'clock sharp no matter how I felt. Lay awake nights for fear I wouldn't get that contract. Used to worry about the world, too. Got all worked up about whether Cleveland or Blaine was going to be elected President—seemed awful important at the time, but who cares now? What I'm trying to say, Mr. Kirby, is that I've had thirty-five years that nobody can take away from me, no matter what they do to the world. See?

KIRBY. (*Crossing to table.*) Yes, I do see. And it's a very dangerous philosophy, Mr. Vanderhof. It's—it's un-American. And it's exactly *why* I'm opposed to this marriage. (ALICE *turns.*) I don't want Tony to come under its influence.

TONY. (*Crossing down from buffet. A gleam in his eye.*) What's the matter with it, Father?

KIRBY. Matter with it? Why, it's—it's downright Communism, that's what it is. (*Crosses* L.)

TONY. You didn't always think so.

KIRBY. I most certainly did. What are you talking about?

TONY. I'll tell you what I'm talking about. You didn't always think so, because there was a time when you wanted to be a trapeze artist. (ALICE *comes down.*)

KIRBY. Why—why, don't be an idiot, Tony.

TONY. Oh, yes, you did. I came across those letters you wrote to Grandfather. Do you remember those?

KIRBY. NO! . . . (*Turns away.*) How dared you read those letters? How dared you?

PENNY. Why, isn't that wonderful? Did you wear tights, Mr. Kirby?

KIRBY. Certainly not! The whole thing is absurd. I was fourteen years old at the time.

TONY. (*Crosses a step.*) Yes, but at *eighteen* you wanted to be a saxophone player, didn't you?

KIRBY. Tony!

TONY. And at twenty-one you ran away from home because Grandfather wanted you to go into the business. It's all down there in black and white. You didn't always think so. (*Crosses* U.S. *to* R.) (ALICE *turns.*)

GRANDPA. Well, well, well!

KIRBY. I may have had silly notions in my youth, but thank God my father knocked them out of me. I went into the business and forgot about them.

TONY. (*Crossing back to* KIRBY.) Not altogether, Father. There's still a saxophone in the back of your clothes closet.

GRANDPA. There is?

KIRBY. (*Quietly.*) That's enough, Tony. We'll discuss this later.

TONY. No, I want to talk about it *now.* I think Mr. Vanderhof is right—dead right. I'm never going back to that office. I've always hated it, and I'm not going on with it. And I'll tell you something else. (ED *starts down the stairs and crosses down to* PENNY.) I didn't make a mistake last night. I knew it was the wrong night. I brought you here on purpose.

76

ALICE. Tony!

PENNY. Well, for heaven's ——

TONY. Because I wanted to wake you up. I wanted you to see a real family—as they really *were*. A family that loved and understood each other. You don't understand *me*. You've never had time. Well, I'm not going to make *your* mistake. I'm clearing out.

KIRBY. Clearing out? What do you mean?

TONY. I mean I'm not going to be pushed into the business just because I'm your son. I'm getting out while there's still time.

KIRBY. But, Tony, what are you going to do?

TONY. I don't know. Maybe I'll be a bricklayer, but at least I'll be doing something *I want to do.* (*Door bell.*)

PENNY. That must be the cab.

GRANDPA. (*Rises and crosses a step to the* R.) Ask him to wait a minute, Ed. (ED *exits hall door* U.L.)

ALICE. Grandpa!

GRANDPA. Do you mind, Alice? (ALICE *goes to alcove—press— back to group.* GRANDPA *rises, crosses up to* TONY.) You know, Mr. Kirby, Tony is going through just what you and I did when we were his age. I think if you listen hard enough you can hear yourself saying the same things to *your* father twenty-five years ago. We all did it. And we were right. How many of us would be willing to settle when we're young for what we eventually get? All those plans we make . . . what happens to them? It's only a handful of the lucky ones that can look back and say that they even came close. (ALICE *turns.* GRANDPA *has hit home.* KIRBY *turns slowly to look at his son, as though seeing him for the first time.* GRANDPA *continues.*) So . . . before they clean out that closet, Mr. Kirby, I think I'd get in a few good hours on that saxophone. (*Comes down to his chair.*) (ED *returns* U.L. *A slight pause after* KIRBY'S *business.* GRAND DUCHESS, *an apron over her evening dress, comes in from kitchen* U.R.)

GRAND DUCHESS. I beg your pardon, but before I make the blintzes, how many will there be for dinner?

GRANDPA. Your Highness, may I present Mr. Anthony Kirby, and Mr. Kirby, Jr.? The Grand Duchess Olga Katrina.

KIRBY. How's that?

GRAND DUCHESS. How do you do? Before I make the blintzes, how many will there be to dinner?

GRANDPA. Oh, I'd make quite a stack of them, Your Highness. Can't ever tell.

GRAND DUCHESS. Good! The Czar always said to me, Olga, do not be stingy with the blintzes. (*She returns to kitchen* U.R. *leaving a somewhat stunned* KIRBY *behind her.*) GRANDPA *laughs, crosses* D.R.)

KIRBY. Ah . . . who did you say that was, Mr. Vanderhof?

GRANDPA. (*Very offhand. Comes down to below table.*) The Grand Duchess Olga Katrina. She's cooking the dinner.

KIRBY. Oh!

GRANDPA. And speaking of dinner, Mr. Kirby, why don't you and Tony both stay?

PENNY. Oh, please do, Mr. Kirby. We've got all that stuff we were going to have last night. I mean tonight.

GRANDPA. (*Sits* R. *of table.*) Looks like a pretty good dinner, Mr. Kirby, and'll kind of give us a chance to get acquainted. Why not stay?

TONY. How about it, Father? Are we staying for dinner?

KIRBY. (*Shifting.*) Why, if you'd care to, Tony, I'd like to, very much.

TONY. (*Crossing up to* ALICE.) Now if Alice will send away that cab, Mr. Vanderhof . . .

GRANDPA. How about it, Alice? Going to be a nice crowd. (ALICE *starts down.*) Don't you think you ought to stay for dinner? (ALICE *is hesitant.*)

KIRBY. I'm staying, Alice. The families ought to get to know each other, don't you think?

ALICE. Mr. Kirby . . . Tony . . . oh, Tony!

TONY. Darling. (*They embrace.*)

ALICE. (*Crossing down and kissing* GRANDPA.) Grandpa, you're wonderful!

GRANDPA. I've been telling you that for years.

ESSIE. (*Entering from kitchen* U.R., *carrying letter and butter dish. She crosses down to* GRANDPA.) Grandpa, here's a letter for you. It was in the icebox.

GRANDPA. Let me see. (*Looking at envelope.*) The Government again.

ESSIE. How do you do, Mr. Kirby?

KIRBY. How do you do?

TONY. (*Crossing to* R. *with* ALICE.) Won't you step into the office, Miss Sycamore? I'd like to do a little dictating.

ED. I'd better tell that cab. (*Exits* U.L.)

GRANDPA. Well, well, well! (ED *enters* U.L.)

78

PENNY. (*Crossing to table.*) What is it, Grandpa?

GRANDPA. The United States Government apologizes. I don't owe 'em a nickel; it seems I died eight years ago. (ED *crosses to* C. *of buffet.*)

ESSIE. Why, what do they mean, Grandpa?

GRANDPA. Remember Charlie, the milkman? Buried under my name?

PENNY. Yes.

GRANDPA. Well, I just told them they made a mistake and I was Martin Vanderhof, Jr. So they're very sorry and I may even get a refund. (ED *crosses to xylophone.*)

ALICE. Why, Grandpa, you're an old crook. (*She crosses up to alcove with* TONY.)

GRANDPA. Sure!

KIRBY. (*Interested.*) Pardon me, how did you say you escaped the income tax, Mr. Vanderhof?

KOL. (*Bursting through kitchen door, bringing a chair with him.*) Tonight, my friends, you are going to eat . . . (*He stops short as he catches sight of* KIRBY.)

KIRBY. (*Heartily.*) Hello, there!

KOL. (*Stunned.*) How do you do?

KIRBY. Fine! Fine! Glad to see you!

KOL. (*To* GRANDPA.) What has happened?

GRANDPA. He's relaxing. (ED *strikes keys of xylophone.*) That's right, play something, Ed. ED *starts to play.* ESSIE *is immediately up on her toes as* KOLENKHOV *goes up to xylophone and sings "Goody-Goody!"* PENNY *applauds.* KIRBY *joins group at xylophone.*)

GRAND DUCHESS. (*Entering from kitchen.*) Everything will be ready in a minute. You can sit down.

PENNY. (*Pulling her desk chair over.*) Come on, everybody. Dinner! (*They start to pull up chairs.*) Come on, Mr. Kirby! (DE PINNA *enters from kitchen.*)

KIRBY. (*Still interested in xylophone.*) Yes, yes, I'm coming.

PENNY. Essie, stop dancing and come to dinner. (ESSIE *brings a chair from hall, dances to table.*)

KOL. You will like Russian food, Mr. Kirby.

PENNY. But you must be careful of your indigestion.

KIRBY. Nonsense! I haven't any indigestion.

TONY. Well, Miss Sycamore, how was your trip to the Adirondacks?

ALICE. Shut your face, Mr. Kirby.

KOL. In Russia when they sit down to dinner . . .

GRANDPA. (*Tapping on his plate.*) Quiet! everybody! Quiet! (*Immediately the talk ceases. All heads are lowered as* GRANDPA *starts to say Grace.*) Well, Sir, here we are again. We want to say thanks once more for everything You've done for us. Things seem to be going along fine. Alice is going to marry Tony, and it looks as if they're going to be very happy. Of course the fireworks blew up, but that was Mr. De Pinna's fault, (DE PINNA *raises his head.*) not Yours. We've all got our health and as far as anything else is concerned we'll leave it to You. Thank You. (*The heads come up again.* RHEBA *and* DONALD *in fresh uniforms come through kitchen door with a goose on a large platter and a huge stack of blintzes.*)

KOL. Grandpa, I have heard from my friend in Siberia. (*Curtain starts down.*) He has escaped again!

GRANDPA. Save the stamp for me!

PENNY. (*On the cue "*. . . *friend in Siberia."*) Mr. Kirby, do you like roast goose? We have roast goose for dinner.

KIRBY. Like it? Why, it's my favorite dish.

ESSIE. Mr. Kirby, I'm going to dance for you later. I've got a new mazurka.

ED. I've written some special music for it.

DE PINNA. Tell me, Mr. Kirby . . . what do you think of The Securities Commission?

PAUL. Mr. De Pinna, we've got to start thinking about next year's fireworks.

ALICE. Well, here goes the Adirondacks.

TONY. And a very good thing, too.

CURTAIN

STAGE DIAGRAM

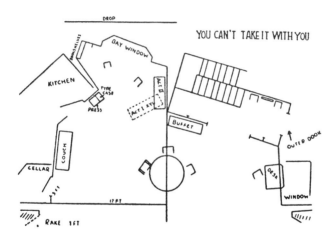

YOU CAN'T TAKE IT WITH YOU

PROPERTY PLOT

ACT I—SCENE I

Wastebasket—D.S. of desk
Desk—L.C. at window
  Typewriter
    2 sheets partly typed paper
    Carbon
  2 kittens on manuscript paper D.S.
  Pile of manuscript paper typed
    D.S.
  Saucer of milk
  Pile of clean paper
  Skull ash tray with candy
    Candy
  Pencil container
    12 pencils
  10 pads
  Blotter pad under typewriter
    Blotter
  Hand blotter
  Eraser
  File box U.S.L.
    Typed papers and carbons
  China inkwell
  Inkwell stand
    2 inkwells
    Pens
  Memo pad
  Calendar
  Bill sticker
  Pile magazines and newspapers
    D.S.L.
  Pile manuscripts U.S.R.
  Dish towel—lower drawer D.S.
    end
Desk chair
  Cushion
Hatrack—hall below stairs
  Raincoat—U.D. hook L.S.
  Rubbers
  Pile of letters—shelf
  Chinese robe—2nd hook R. side
  Woman's umbrella
  Man's umbrella

Cane
Blue chair—L. of hatrack
Blue chair—off R. of hall
Buffet—U.C. between alcove and
  arch
  Snake solarium—C.
  Folded white tablecloth in drawer
    top R.
  Phone—L. end
  Pile magazines and newspapers
    under phone
  Pile of magazines—R. end
    Cupid statue
  Pile of magazines R. of solarium
  Fancy box—U.L. corner
  Silver tray
  Small head (bearded man)—L.
    solarium
Table—C.
  Mat
  Table cover
  Japanese flower bowl
Armchair—R. of table
Red chair—L. of table
Red chair—above table
Xylophone—R. of alcove
  Xylophone hammers
Bookcase—U.L. of alcove
  Top shelf
    Pile of magazines
    Statue of Washington
    Egyptian statue
    Small picture
    Small vase
    Vase
    Venus statue
  Wooden plate
  3rd shelf
    Tom-toms
    Crocodile stuffed
  Chinamug shell

2nd shelf
Stamp album (loose stamps)
Pile of magazines (box of xylophone sticks)
Bottom shelf
Pile of newspapers
Slippers—floor R. of bookcase L.
Bookcase—U.R. of alcove
Top shelf
Plaster foot
Pile of magazines
2 Oriental candlesticks
Palette
Pottery vase
Small blue vase
Samovar
Ash tray
Bookcase—U.R. of alcove
Blue white vase—3rd shelf
Pile magazines—2nd shelf top of books
Pile newspapers—bottom shelf top of books

Fern stand—U.C. alcove
Fern vase
Fern
2 piles newspapers on floor L. and R. of fern
Picture, religious—on floor R. of fern
Table—D.R. of alcove
Hand press
Type case
Type
3 sheets paper
Ink roller
Steel case for paper
Paper
Type stick on steel case
Inlaid chair—U.S. of kitchen door
Pile of magazines and newspapers
2 pictures—fish
Couch—R.C.
2 cushions
Couch cover
Ship—hung center of alcove arch

ON STAGE PROPS

2 small pictures—D.S.L. below window
Shield—floor D.L. against wall
1 small picture—U.S.L. above window
Fire shield—U.L. corner
Shelf—U.L. corner
Statue—2 women nude
2 gilt framed pictures—wall L. of arch
2 small pictures below 2 gilt pictures
2 pictures—hall L. of hatrack
Large picture—hall R. of hatrack
Picture—wall above stairs
Small picture—L. of solarium
Plaster picture—R. of solarium
2 pictures—small—above snake solarium
Large fancy plate—hung over buffet C.
What-not shelf—above buffet—L. of big plate

Openwork vase
Flowers
Tusk—hung above R. end of buffet
Small gilt picture (ship) above R. end of buffet
Small picture L. of tusk over buffet
Medal hung under what-not shelf C.
2 small pictures over buffet—L. of big plate
Bell pull L. of arch U.L.
Horsewoman statue on floor L. of buffet
3 pictures D.S. of bracket L. of alcove
Unframed oval painting on bracket L. of alcove
Picture—wood—against L.U. corner wall
Gilt picture (woman—dress half) against L. bookcase
Chinese girl picture against L. wall of alcove

83

2 pictures—above bookcase L.
2 pictures—above bookcase R.
Picture—R. wall of alcove
Fly whip—hung above hand press
Silhouette picture—wall R. above U.S. door
Long narrow picture—over R.U.S. door
Bird frame—below bracket R.
Basket on bracket R.
Oriental mask hung on bracket R.
Long picture—D.S. of door U.R. jog
Small silhouette picture—above long picture
Small gilt picture—(2 women) U.R. above door above silhouette

Picture over bracket R.
Picture—U.S. of bracket R.
2 small pictures—above couch R.
Vase—window sill L.
Small picture—above window at shelf
Japanese carved border—bay window U.R.
Curtains—bay window U.R.
Curtain and drapes—window L.
Stained glass piece—hung in window L.
Plaque—over arch U.L.
Velvet curtains—arch U.L.
Carpet

OFF U.R.

8 dinner plates (Rheba)
  Salt and pepper shakers on 8 plates
Plate of cocoanut marshmallow candy—8 pieces (Essie)
8 forks ⎫
8 knives ⎪
8 spoons ⎬ (Rheba)
8 napkins ⎪
Towel ⎭

Jar of flies (small) (Rheba)
Plate of 3 tomatoes (Rheba)
Platter of sliced watermelon (Rheba)
Platter of spaghetti and meatballs (Rheba)
Platter of corn on cob (Donald)
Small tray (silver)
  Bowl of corn flakes

BASEMENT

Bass drum, cushion and lath

OFF L.

Business card (Henderson)
Manila envelope (Henderson)
  Copies of income tax letters

Trotzky book (Paul)
Jar of flies (4 oz.) (Donald)

OFF D.R.

Metal plate (Paul)
Small firecrackers (practical)
Cigarettes (Paul)

Matches (Paul)
2 large firecrackers (De Pinna)
2 skyrockets (De Pinna)

PERSONAL PROPS

Pipe, tobacco and matches (De Pinna)

ACT I—SCENE I

Center table
  Tablecloth
  7 plates
  7 forks
  7 knives
  7 napkins
  Plate of tomatoes
  Plate of candy
  Platter of spaghetti

Platter of corn on cob
Desk chair cushion
Hat on newel post
Xylophone
Album on floor—armchair R. of
  table
Grandpa's shoes, coat and Hender-
  son's hat

ACT I—SCENE II

Table—C.
  Table cover
  Tall vase with flowers

Buffet
  Skull with candy—R. end

OFF U.R.

Bottle Whiterock ⎫ **Tony**
Bottle opener ⎭

2 glasses (Alice)
Accordion (Donald)

ACT II

Desk—L. of window
  Typewriter
  Skull
  File box
  Typed sheets, carbons
  Blotter pad
  Blotter
  Hand blotter
  Inkwell tray
  2 pens
  Pencils
  Shell container for pencils
    12 pencils
  Pile of magazines, newspapers
  8 pads U.S. of typewriter
  2 pads, 2 pencils on manuscripts
    U.S.
  Manuscripts D.S. end
  Ash tray
  Typed script sheets D.S. end
  Glass of water D.S. end
Desk chair—(cushion is dead after
  Act I, Scene I)
Buffet—
  Erector ship—R. end

Mast—R. end
British flag—R. end
Snake solarium—C.
Target—R. end behind ship
6 darts—R. end behind ship
Jap flower garden bowl—L. end
Phone—L. end
Pile of magazines—R. end
Pile of magazines—L. end
Plaster head (bearded man)—R.
  end
Fancy box—R. end
Table—C.
  Tablecloth
  3 coffee cups (used)
  3 saucers
  3 spoons
  6 napkins (rumpled)
  Glass—U.R. side
  Bottle of gin (no cap) ⎫ L. side
  Small glass ⎭
Tray—on stage at rise (Donald)
  6 dessert dishes
  6 spoons
  2 glasses

85

1 cup
1 saucer
1 spoon
Armchair—R. of table
  Newspaper—(*N.Y. Post*)
Desk chair—D.S. of table
Red chair—L. of table
Red chair—above table
Xylophone—U. and D. stage
  Xylophone hammers
2 chairs
Alcove

Couch
  2 cushions
  Cover—D.S. end
Press table
  Mask
Hatrack—hall
  Gay's hat—Grandpa's hat—
    Henderson's hat
Chair—L. of hatrack
Chair—hall off R.
Stamp album—bookcase U.L. of
  alcove
Inlaid chair—U.R. below hand press

OFF U.R.

Tray (Rheba)
Candy boxes tied together (Ed)

Tray (Donald)
Table cover (Donald)

OFF D.R.

Painting (De Pinna)
Easel (De Pinna)
Model platform (De Pinna)
Stove lid (De Pinna)

Racing Form (De Pinna)
Coat (wardrobe on hook) (De
  Pinna)

OFF L.

3 filled grocery bags (Donald)
4 printed circulars (1st G-Man)

Package of eggs (Donald)

OFF U.C. ON PLATFORM

Palette, brushes and paint box (Penny)

PERSONAL PROPS

Eyeglasses (Kirby)
Pipe and tobacco (De Pinna)
Matches (De Pinna)
Government letter—opened
  (Grandpa)

Stamp (Kolenkhov)
Case and cigarettes (Kolenkhov)
Small wrench, for Meccano set
  (Paul)

ACT III

Desk—L.
  (Leave props same as end of Act
  II)
Desk chair

Buffet
  (Same as end of Act II)
  7 salad plates—7 forks
  Table cover

Table—c.
Opened newspaper with typed
  speech (Donald)
3 plates (set) D.S. end
3 forks (set) D.S. end
3 knives (set) D.S. end
2 darts—D.S. end
1 dart—U.S. end
3 napkins—(set)
White tablecloth
Carving set—R. side

Pile of 4 plates
Pile of 4 knives, 4 forks
Pile of 4 napkins
Salt and pepper shakers
Xylophone
  2 soft sticks
  1 hard stick
Couch—R.
  Same as end of Act II
Hand press table
  Same as end of Act II

OFF U.R.

Sealed government letter (Essie)
Tray (Donald)
  Roast goose

Tray (Rheba)
Blintzes

OFF D.R.

Bandages—adhesive (De Pinna)

OFF U.R.

Butter dish (Essie)

2 kitchen chairs

OFF L.

2 prop dresses (wardrobe, Alice)—
  on platform

Dressing case ⎫
Hatbox   ⎬ (Ed) on platform
Big suitcase (Ed) on platform

87

NEW PLAYS

★ **THE CREDEAUX CANVAS by Keith Bunin.** A forged painting leads to tragedy among friends. "There is that moment between adolescence and middle age when being disaffected looks attractive. Witness the enduring appeal of Prince Hamlet, Jake Barnes and James Dean, on the stage, page and screen. Or, more immediately, take a look at the lithe young things in THE CREDEAUX CANVAS…" –*NY Times.* "THE CREDEAUX CANVAS is the third recent play about painters…it turned out to be the best of the lot, better even than most plays about non-painters." –*NY Magazine.* [2M, 2W] ISBN: 0-8222-1838-0

★ **THE DIARY OF ANNE FRANK by Frances Goodrich and Albert Hackett, newly adapted by Wendy Kesselman.** A transcendently powerful new adaptation in which Anne Frank emerges from history a living, lyrical, intensely gifted young girl. "Undeniably moving. It shatters the heart. The evening never lets us forget the inhuman darkness waiting to claim its incandescently human heroine." –*NY Times.* "A sensitive, stirring and thoroughly engaging new adaptation." –*NY Newsday.* "A powerful new version that moves the audience to gasps, then tears." –*A.P.* "One of the year's ten best." –*Time Magazine.* [5M, 5W, 3 extras] ISBN: 0-8222-1718-X

★ **THE BOOK OF LIZ by David Sedaris and Amy Sedaris.** Sister Elizabeth Donderstock makes the cheese balls that support her religious community, but feeling unappreciated among the Squeamish, she decides to try her luck in the outside world. "…[a] delightfully off-key, off-color hymn to clichés we all live by, whether we know it or not." –*NY Times.* "Good-natured, goofy and frequently hilarious…" –*NY Newsday.* "…[THE BOOK OF LIZ] may well be the world's first Amish picaresque…hilarious…" –*Village Voice.* [2M, 2W (doubling, flexible casting to 8M, 7W)] ISBN: 0-8222-1827-5

★ **JAR THE FLOOR by Cheryl L. West.** A quartet of black women spanning four generations makes up this hilarious and heartwarming dramatic comedy. "…a moving and hilarious account of a black family sparring in a Chicago suburb…" –*NY Magazine.* "…heart-to-heart confrontations and surprising revelations…first-rate…" –*NY Daily News.* "…unpretentious good feelings…bubble through West's loving and humorous play…" –*Star-Ledger.* "…one of the wisest plays I've seen in ages…[from] a master playwright." –*USA Today.* [5W] ISBN: 0-8222-1809-7

★ **THIEF RIVER by Lee Blessing.** Love between two men over decades is explored in this incisive portrait of coming to terms with who you are. "Mr. Blessing unspools the plot ingeniously, skipping back and forth in time as the details require…an absorbing evening." –*NY Times.* "…wistful and sweet-spirited…" –*Variety.* [6M] ISBN: 0-8222-1839-9

★ **THE BEGINNING OF AUGUST by Tom Donaghy.** When Jackie's wife abruptly and mysteriously leaves him and their infant daughter, a pungently comic reevaluation of suburban life ensues. "Donaghy holds a cracked mirror up to the contemporary American family, anatomizing its frailties and miscommunications in fractured language that can be both funny and poignant." –*The Philadelphia Inquirer.* "…[A] sharp, eccentric new comedy. Pungently funny…fresh and precise…" –*LA Times.* [3M, 2W] ISBN: 0-8222-1786-4

★ **OUTSTANDING MEN'S MONOLOGUES 2001–2002 and OUTSTANDING WOMEN'S MONOLOGUES 2001–2002 edited by Craig Pospisil.** Drawn exclusively from Dramatists Play Service publications, these collections for actors feature over fifty monologues each and include an enormous range of voices, subject matter and characters. MEN'S ISBN: 0-8222-1821-6 WOMEN'S ISBN: 0-8222-1822-4

DRAMATISTS PLAY SERVICE, INC.
440 Park Avenue South, New York, NY 10016 212-683-8960 Fax 212-213-1539
postmaster@dramatists.com www.dramatists.com

NEW PLAYS

★ **A LESSON BEFORE DYING by Romulus Linney, based on the novel by Ernest J. Gaines.** An innocent young man is condemned to death in backwoods Louisiana and must learn to die with dignity. "The story's wrenching power lies not in its outrage but in the almost inexplicable grace the characters must muster as their only resistance to being treated like lesser beings." *–The New Yorker.* "Irresistible momentum and a cathartic explosion...a powerful inevitability." *–NY Times.* [5M, 2W] ISBN: 0-8222-1785-6

★ **BOOM TOWN by Jeff Daniels.** A searing drama mixing small-town love, politics and the consequences of betrayal. "...a brutally honest, contemporary foray into classic themes, exploring what moves people to lie, cheat, love and dream. By BOOM TOWN's climactic end there are no secrets, only bare truth." *–Oakland Press.* "...some of the most electrifying writing Daniels has ever done..." *–Ann Arbor News.* [2M, 1W] ISBN: 0-8222-1760-0

★ **INCORRUPTIBLE by Michael Hollinger.** When a motley order of medieval monks learns their patron saint no longer works miracles, a larcenous, one-eyed minstrel shows them an outrageous new way to pay old debts. "A lightning-fast farce, rich in both verbal and physical humor." *–American Theatre.* "Everything fits snugly in this funny, endearing black comedy...an artful blend of the mock-formal and the anachronistically breezy...A piece of remarkably dexterous craftsmanship." *–Philadelphia Inquirer.* "A farcical romp, scintillating and irreverent." *–Philadelphia Weekly.* [5M, 3W] ISBN: 0-8222-1787-2

★ **CELLINI by John Patrick Shanley.** Chronicles the life of the original "Renaissance Man," Benvenuto Cellini, the sixteenth-century Italian sculptor and man-about-town. Adapted from the autobiography of Benvenuto Cellini, translated by J. Addington Symonds. "[Shanley] has created a convincing Cellini, not neglecting his dark side, and a trim, vigorous, fast-moving show." *–BackStage.* "Very entertaining...With brave purpose, the narrative undermines chronology before untangling it...touching and funny..." *–NY Times.* [7M, 2W (doubling)] ISBN: 0-8222-1808-9

★ **PRAYING FOR RAIN by Robert Vaughan.** Examines a burst of fatal violence and its aftermath in a suburban high school. "Thought provoking and compelling." *–Denver Post.* "Vaughan's powerful drama offers hope and possibilities." *–Theatre.com.* "[The play] doesn't put forth compact, tidy answers to the problem of youth violence. What it does offer is a compelling exploration of the forces that influence an individual's choices, and of the proverbial lifelines—be they familial, communal, religious or political—that tragically slacken when society gives in to apathy, fear and self-doubt..." *–Westword.* "...a symphony of anger..." *–Gazette Telegraph.* [4M, 3W] ISBN: 0-8222-1807-0

★ **GOD'S MAN IN TEXAS by David Rambo.** When a young pastor takes over one of the most prestigious Baptist churches from a rip-roaring old preacher-entrepreneur, all hell breaks loose. "...the pick of the litter of all the works at the Humana Festival..." *–Providence Journal.* "...a wealth of both drama and comedy in the struggle for power..." *–LA Times.* "...the first act is so funny...deepens in the second act into a sobering portrait of fear, hope and self-delusion..." *–Columbus Dispatch.* [3M] ISBN: 0-8222-1801-1

★ **JESUS HOPPED THE 'A' TRAIN by Stephen Adly Guirgis.** A probing, intense portrait of lives behind bars at Rikers Island. "...fire-breathing...whenever it appears that JESUS is settling into familiar territory, it slides right beneath expectations into another, fresher direction. It has the courage of its intellectual restlessness...[JESUS HOPPED THE 'A' TRAIN] has been written in flame." *–NY Times.* [4M, 1W] ISBN: 0-8222-1799-6

DRAMATISTS PLAY SERVICE, INC.
440 Park Avenue South, New York, NY 10016 212-683-8960 Fax 212-213-1539
postmaster@dramatists.com www.dramatists.com

NEW PLAYS

★ **THE CIDER HOUSE RULES, PARTS 1 & 2 by Peter Parnell, adapted from the novel by John Irving.** Spanning eight decades of American life, this adaptation from the Irving novel tells the story of Dr. Wilbur Larch, founder of the St. Cloud's, Maine orphanage and hospital, and of the complex father-son relationship he develops with the young orphan Homer Wells. "...luxurious digressions, confident pacing...an enterprise of scope and vigor..." –*NY Times.* "...The fact that I can't wait to see Part 2 only begins to suggest just how good it is..." –*NY Daily News.* "...engrossing...an odyssey that has only one major shortcoming: It comes to an end." –*Seattle Times.* "...outstanding...captures the humor, the humility...of Irving's 588-page novel..." –*Seattle Post-Intelligencer.* [9M, 10W, doubling, flexible casting] PART 1 ISBN: 0-8222-1725-2 PART 2 ISBN: 0-8222-1726-0

★ **TEN UNKNOWNS by Jon Robin Baitz.** An iconoclastic American painter in his seventies has his life turned upside down by an art dealer and his ex-boyfriend. "...breadth and complexity...a sweet and delicate harmony rises from the four cast members...Mr. Baitz is without peer among his contemporaries in creating dialogue that spontaneously conveys a character's social context and moral limitations..." –*NY Times.* "...darkly funny, brilliantly desperate comedy...TEN UNKNOWNS vibrates with vital voices." –*NY Post.* [3M, 1W] ISBN: 0-8222-1826-7

★ **BOOK OF DAYS by Lanford Wilson.** A small-town actress playing St. Joan struggles to expose a murder. "...[Wilson's] best work since *Fifth of July*...An intriguing, prismatic and thoroughly engrossing depiction of contemporary small-town life with a murder mystery at its core...a splendid evening of theater..." –*Variety.* "...fascinating...a densely populated, unpredictable little world." –*St. Louis Post-Dispatch.* [6M, 5W] ISBN: 0-8222-1767-8

★ **THE SYRINGA TREE by Pamela Gien.** Winner of the 2001 Obie Award. A breathtakingly beautiful tale of growing up white in apartheid South Africa. "Instantly engaging, exotic, complex, deeply shocking...a thoroughly persuasive transport to a time and a place...stun[s] with the power of a gut punch..." –*NY Times.* "Astonishing...affecting ...[with] a dramatic and heartbreaking conclusion...A deceptive sweet simplicity haunts THE SYRINGA TREE..." –*A.P.* [1W (or flexible cast)] ISBN: 0-8222-1792-9

★ **COYOTE ON A FENCE by Bruce Graham.** An emotionally riveting look at capital punishment. "The language is as precise as it is profane, provoking both troubling thought and the occasional cheerful laugh...will change you a little before it lets go of you." –*Cincinnati CityBeat.* "...excellent theater in every way..." –*Philadelphia City Paper.* [3M, 1W] ISBN: 0-8222-1738-4

★ **THE PLAY ABOUT THE BABY by Edward Albee.** Concerns a young couple who have just had a baby and the strange turn of events that transpire when they are visited by an older man and woman. "An invaluable self-portrait of sorts from one of the few genuinely great living American dramatists...rockets into that special corner of theater heaven where words shoot off like fireworks into dazzling patterns and hues." –*NY Times.* "An exhilarating, wicked...emotional terrorism." –*NY Newsday.* [2M, 2W] ISBN: 0-8222-1814-3

★ **FORCE CONTINUUM by Kia Corthron.** Tensions among black and white police officers and the neighborhoods they serve form the backdrop of this discomfiting look at life in the inner city. "The creator of this intense...new play is a singular voice among American playwrights...exceptionally eloquent..." –*NY Times.* "...a rich subject and a wise attitude." –*NY Post.* [6M, 2W, 1 boy] ISBN: 0-8222-1817-8

DRAMATISTS PLAY SERVICE, INC.
440 Park Avenue South, New York, NY 10016 212-683-8960 Fax 212-213-1539
postmaster@dramatists.com www.dramatists.com